A Bouquet of Memories:
Reminiscences of Eighty Years

Further copies of this book can be ordered
online securely using a credit card at:

www.theotokos.org.uk/pages/books/books.html

or you can order copies via online booksellers,
or through your local bookseller.

A Bouquet of Memories: Reminiscences of Eighty Years

Mary Goodhind

Theotokos Books

Published by Theotokos Books
Nottingham, England

www.theotokos.org.uk
books@theotokos.org.uk

First Published in 2013

Cover design/implemenation by Mike Daley

ISBN 978-0-9574969-0-3

Contents

Preface

When our grandchildren started to ask questions about World War II—because they were learning about it in school—I realised that every year there are fewer and fewer people alive who actually lived through the War. Not only that, there are even fewer who are still able to write about their experiences. So it was initially for the benefit of our eight grandchildren and four children that the first part of this book was written, and although it is not intended to be a history of the war, there are some statistics taken from the newspapers of the day.

The second part of the book is just memories of some of the things that I did as a young woman. Even our children might be surprised at what I got up to. Our youngest son has described it as "compelling reading." I hope he is right.

1

How it all Began

When World War II was declared in September 1939, I was just seven years old and my brother Rory was nine. We were living with our parents in Forest Gate, a part of East London. By today's standards we were really quite poor, managing on just three pounds a week. Our father worked at Woolwich Arsenal examining detonators. He had been in the Navy when World War I came to an end and considered himself fortunate to have a job at all. I don't think our parents would have considered themselves poor, although they couldn't afford to rent or buy a house locally, so we shared a house with two single ladies.

My first home was a terraced house in Forest Gate, on the edge of London's East End, overlooking Plashet Park. I was born on 8th May 1932, in the front bedroom of a house in Lincoln Road. It was one of two rooms rented by my parents, Eleanor and Thomas McDermott, (known as Nell and Tom). My brother Rory was two years old at the time and until he was five years old, we all shared the same bedroom. Our living room was downstairs at the back of the house and from the window we could see the garden and beyond that, Plashet Park. We shared the kitchen and the toilet with the other occupants of the house, two single sisters who were, in fact, the tenants. Florrie and Alice Alford had grown up in that house, the owner being another lady who had flatly refused to have electricity installed. Hence the rooms were lit by gaslight and heated by coal fires.

My Father in the 1920s

The kitchen was very basic, but probably no more so than many other kitchens in the 1930s. We had a gas cooker, a brick-built copper boiler and a shallow stone sink. There was no hot-water system, just a cold water tap. When we needed hot water, it was boiled up on the cooker or in the copper. Beneath the window in the kitchen was a semi-circular table. The back door of the house led from the kitchen into a lean-to, and at one end of the lean-to was the toilet. We were fortunate in that we did not have to go outside to the toilet, although it was actually outside the house. We did not have a bathroom so we bathed in a zinc bath in our living area. When not in use the bath hung on the garden fence. The kitchen was painted dark green, and on one of the walls hung a long wooden plaque on which was written in black paint, the Lord's Prayer.

Our living room was very small but also very cosy. When we eventually moved, in February 1940, the removal men could not believe that so much furniture could be crammed into so small a space. The fireplace was a kitchen range, so a certain amount of cooking was done in the oven when the fire was alight. On one side of the fireplace there was a built-in dresser and on the other side a ceiling to floor cupboard.

We had a small gate-leg table and four Polish wooden chairs with round seats and round backs and also one larger chair of the same design with arms. To this day I have that chair. Another relic of those days that only went when my late mother's house was sold was a wooden armchair that had been "cut down" to make a suitable nursing chair, when we were babies. It gave our mother a good lap on which to change our nappies. Our father, Thomas, was a prolific reader, so we had a very large bookcase crammed full of everything from Agatha Christie to G. K. Chesterton and Charles Dickens—we had a very large set of his books given to us by our grandfather.

We also had a treadle sewing machine, an essential piece of equipment as Mother made many of our clothes, having been in the needlework trade before she was married. When my maternal grandmother died, we inherited her piano, and somehow that was also incorporated into the tiny living room.

The floor was covered with lino, with a coconut mat in front of the fire. Our father was a great story teller and in the winter we would sit for hours in front of the fire, listening to fairy stories that he made up as he went along. On the dresser we had an accumulator wireless, which had a battery that we took to the bicycle shop to be recharged. Rory and I were avid listeners of "Children's Hour."

Perhaps the thing that I remember most about living in Lincoln Road was the park at the bottom of the garden. Separated by only a low railing at the bottom of our garden, we spent many happy hours in that park, on initially, Rory's little blue Kiddie-car and our three-wheelers, and then our fairy-cycles, before we graduated to real bikes. Although by today's standards I suppose we would be considered deprived, but

Rory and myself on our bikes in Plashet Park in 1938

compared with many of the children who came to play with us in the park we were well off.

Every now and again we would turn out our toy cupboard and fill some carrier bags with the unwanted toys and give them away to children in the park. I even gave my three-wheeled bike to a little boy who admired it.

We knew many regular visitors to the park—the people who walked their dogs; "grandad", a veteran of WW I, who held a kind of "Kite Club" in a corner of the tennis courts; the cricketers who played every Saturday afternoon during the summer on the green nearest our garden; and many children who talked and played with us because we were always there.

Those halcyon days came to an end with the outbreak of the Second World War, when we moved south of the river, partly for safety and partly to be closer to our father's place of work. My memories of these years before the War are of a sort of Garden of Eden, where sorrow and unhappiness had not reached us and war was just a word. To our parents, however, the horrors of the First World War were only a short time in the past. When the possibility of another war became a reality it must have been too terrible for them to contemplate.

Rory, my Father, and myself
In Plashet Park In 1935

During the year before war was declared things began to happen that indicated that in all probability there would be another conflict. A team of men came round and installed air raid shelters in our back garden. Search lights were tried out at night and air raid sirens tested during the day. Guns boomed out across the River Thames where Woolwich Arsenal was situated.

At school our teachers prepared us for evacuation by painting a rosy picture of life in the country with foster parents.

So why did we have to go to war? After the experience of the Great War (as the First World War was called) it was not something to be entered into lightly. In November 1932, the

Prime Minister, Stanley Baldwin, told the House of Commons "I think it is well for the man in the street to realise that there is no power on earth that can protect him from being bombed".

On the 1st September 1939 we were all in our little living room in Lincoln Road, Forest Gate listening to the "wireless". I was embroidering a picture of a church that my father had drawn on a piece of white cloth. At 10 o'clock it was announced that German troops had invaded Poland. At that moment the lives of millions of people, including that of our little family, changed forever.

My Mother, myself, and Rory in Plashet Park in 1935

My parents must have discussed what they would do in the event of the Germans invading Poland. Rory and I knew nothing about their plans until that morning when we were told that with our mother we would be taken by car to Bognor Regis. The previous day we had seen a stream of children walking past our house on the way to the railway station. They were all being evacuated to places of safety as part of the Government scheme that we had been told about at school.

We had never been away from home, not even for one night and our parents decided that they could not let us go away under the Government scheme. Our Dad thought that London would be bombed that night and that was why we had to leave home immediately with Mother. When Rory and I realised that we were leaving Dad behind we began to cry and it seemed as though we cried for hours. Eventually we were sent out into the garden with a slice of cold fruit pudding; looking over the railings into the park we could see a large number of men busy digging public air-raid shelters.

The barrage balloon that had been based near the park gates was straining at it moorings and the park looked strangely deserted. Most of our little friends had been evacuated, and sadly we were never to see them again.

When we returned to the house a hired car was waiting to take us to Bognor Regis. We said a tearful goodbye to our father and Auntie Alice (with whom we shared the house), and an Irish lady that we called Auntie Molly, who was later killed by a bomb.

It was a long drive to Bognor and once we got over the crying it was a bit of an adventure. Rory had never been in a car before and I had only been on one journey when two teachers had taken me to Brentwood. We passed many groups of men who were digging sand out of the banks on the side of the road to make sandbags.

As we neared our destination I began to feel sick and as happens with little children I brought it up over everything. The one toy that I had been allowed to take, my teddy bear, did not escape and was "out of action" for weeks.

Joe and Win Baillie were friends of my grand-parents and they ran a boarding house in Bognor Regis. They had agreed to take us in if war was declared, so it was to their house (No. 5 Richmond Avenue) that we were heading.

I have read in books about the War that all the towns on the south coast were themselves evacuated. Well I can say that Bognor Regis was not one of these towns. It was over-crowded with evacuees from South London and we shared a house with ten children from Clapham and Balham.

Bearing in mind that the school holidays were not yet over, some of the summer guests were still in residence at Number 5 Richmond Avenue. These were two elderly ladies and a little boy with his aunt who came from Croydon.

We were welcomed by the Baillies with open arms and ushered into a side room where tea was laid out for the three of us. Joe could see that we were inclined to be tearful so he brought his little dog, Girlie, to see us. Girlie (or Josephine as was her real name) did tricks for chocolate buttons. There was another dog Prince, a big Chow. Doing tricks would have been beneath his dignity, and he would only enter the house through the front door.

Win Baillie was a very motherly person although she and Joe did not have any children. Win's sister Lil also lived in the house and helped with the guests. Her fiancée was killed in the First World War and she had never married.

2

Evacuation, and a new House

We left Forest Gate on Friday 1ˢᵗ September but war was not declared until Sunday 3ʳᵈ September. Right up to the last minute our mother was optimistic that there would not be a war. Of course she was wrong; but then she hoped it would be over by Christmas.

In the meantime we settled down to life as evacuees, along with the ten other children from London. We slept in a room with a double and a single bed. In the large room next to ours there were several beds where some of the children slept and the others were in various other rooms. The ages of the children were from 13 to 3 ½, the youngest being little Albert Pim who was evacuated with his older sister, Winnie.

They also had another sister, Joan, who was about eight. Winnie, who was only twelve, had to look after both of the younger children. Their father was a Billingsgate fish monger. I remember him visiting his children on one occasion and he brought some winkles with him that were shared amongst us. It was the only time that I ever tasted winkles but I really enjoyed them.

The food that Win and Joe provided was very good. After all, they were both cooks. We all sat round a large table in the back room that looked out onto the small garden. The three Pim children sat at a separate table. I know we sometimes had a cooked breakfast because I remember having toad in the hole for breakfast. We all came home from school at mid-day for a cooked meal and then had bread and margarine for tea. We were not accustomed to margarine although I suppose the tea was much the same as we had at home.

After the tea was cleared away we had to amuse ourselves until bed time. There was only one boy apart from Rory (and little Albert of course). His name was Ronnie Dent and I think he was ten years old.

It must have been awful for our mother sitting in a room full of children. She did the washing up and got herself some knitting (a thing that she had never done at home). We did not have any toys so we had to invent games to play and things to do.

One of the evacuees, a girl named Gwenneth who was twelve years old, took me under her wing. We bought little rubber dolls and with scraps of wool knitted little outfits for them. It was Gwenneth who really taught me to knit, although I had conquered the basics even before I started school. Gwenneth's mother worked in the Co-op and regularly sent her "tuck boxes". She also had a box of dressing up clothes.

I think I would describe Gwenneth as a "leader" of children. Being so much younger, I followed her all the time much to the concern of my mother. Although she looked after me and kept me amused, I knew that sometimes Gwenneth could be unkind to the other children. Shortly before we left Bognor, Gwenneth confided to me that she cried every night. So she was not the self possessed, confident girl that she appeared to be.

During our short stay in Bognor our father visited us as often as he could. He stayed over at Christmas and of course the War was not over as Mother had hoped. During that time there were no air-raids and evacuees began to drift back to London.

Soon after Christmas, our father developed alopecia. His hair was falling out in clumps and the doctor said it was due to stress. Mother said we must go home but of course there was still the danger of the German bombs so we could not return to Forest Gate. That was how we came to live in Barnehurst.

From the very day that Germany invaded Poland a strict blackout was enforced. Every window had to be blacked out and not a single ray of light was allowed to shine through. An Air Raid Warden walked up and down the road each night looking for faulty blackouts. Sometimes the Baillies would forget to draw the curtain in the toilet and we would hear the warden shouting "Put out that light!"

It was very difficult for many people to black out all their windows, especially the poor and the elderly. Rather than black out all their windows some people would just walk about in the dark. There were many reports of accidents with people falling downstairs or walking into things. When Father returned home after visiting us our mother would walk with him to the bus stop, and she commented on the fact that it was absolutely black outside. Not a street lamp, or car light, or house light anywhere.

Food rationing began on 8th January 1940, but the ration books were distributed well before that. In order to buy foods that were rationed the housewife was obliged to register at a shop of her choice. She had to use her ration books at that shop. The reason for the registration was to enable the shop managers to order sufficient food for their customers. The critical rations per person were as follows: butter 4 oz; sugar 12 oz; and bacon and ham 4 oz per person per week. Meat was rationed from 11th March 1940 to the value of 1/10d per person per week, (about 9p), while jam etc. was rationed from March 1941, at 8 oz per month, and cheese from May 1941. Tea was also eventually rationed, in July 1942 (2 oz), and margarine was limited to 6 oz per week in conjunction with butter. These rations did fluctuate from time to time.

When it was decided that we must all live together again but not in Forest Gate, Father had to find another house in a different district, away from the docks, and the threat of bombing, but within cycling distance of Woolwich Arsenal.

One lunch time, he walked out of the Arsenal gate and boarded the first bus that came along. It was a 696 trolleybus that went to Dartford via Welling, Bexleyheath and Crayford He had no idea where he was going but when the bus stopped at Crayford gas works he got off and started to walk up Old Road. A young man named Jack West was walking in the same direction and they got into conversation. It was a bitterly cold day and the road was covered with snow. Father confided to Jack that he was house hunting. As luck would have it, Jack knew of an empty house a few doors away from where he lived in Inglewood Road. Father walked along with him to see the house and without even looking inside decided to take it. By that time he had been promoted to foreman, so he was able to afford to rent a whole house.

I have never really decided whether it was a good idea for my father to take the house without viewing it first or not. When we returned from Bognor and went with our grandmother to have a look inside we were in for a shock. The house had been empty for some time so all the pipes were frozen and some were cracked. The toilet was cracked and the whole house needed redecorating. The owner was an Anglican vicar and he had lived there himself previously. Then he had moved to Jersey and let the house to some relatives. The Rev. Dentith reduced the rent because it was in such poor condition. In all the years that we subsequently lived there as tenants he never increased the rent and when my father was about to retire he let him buy it outright at a price he could afford. So perhaps it was a good idea after all for Father not to look inside on that January day.

We moved in on a bitterly cold Saturday in February. Our mother's brother Tom arranged the removal. The men who did the job were not really removal men but worked for a firm in the docks named Fairclough. Although we only lived in three rooms the van was absolutely full and we had to leave our mangle behind.

Mother and Rory and I made the journey from Forest Gate to Barnehurst by bus and ferry. Our grandpa travelled in the van with Dad, because he needed help with putting up the beds. The homes built in Inglewood Road in 1930 were very basic. There was no heating system, rooms were heated by coal fires and the only way of heating water was by the geyser in the bathroom. I expect many people bought a water heater for the kitchen but for many years our mother heated up the water on the gas cooker.

When we moved in to 33 Inglewood Road there was a shortage of coal, so the only form of heating we had was an oil stove. We couldn't use the toilet because it was cracked so we had to go to a neighbour's house for that purpose. This went on for weeks and I have no doubt that our mother must have wondered if they had done the right thing in moving.

I remember her cooking some sausages on the oil stove so that she could give our grandfather a meal before he made the long journey back to East Ham.

The following morning we walked to the Catholic Church (St. Mary of the Crays) for the 10.30 Mass. The single aisle church was a stark contrast to the Franciscan Church we had attended in Forest Gate. That was where my parents were married, Rory and I were baptized, made our First Communions, and where Rory was confirmed. Our mother was thoroughly miserable. When Mass was over we wended our way through the groups of people chatting outside when Father spotted a familiar face. Ron Goodhind worked in the Arsenal and was at Mass with his wife Kathleen and their little boy David who was in a pushchair.

Twenty six years later, David and I were married. Was that the reason why Father caught that particular bus and alighted at that particular bus stop and spoke to a complete stranger named Jack West?

The first thing that Mother had to do on Monday morning was register our ration books. In the small shopping centre in Barnehurst, just up the road from 33 Inglewood, there were 4 provision shops (grocers) and two butchers. One would have thought that Mother would have registered with one of those shops, but no, she chose a shop called Goodworth's in Bexleyheath. She did however register with the Co-op butcher.

Every week she would leave a list at Goodworth's and a boy would bring the order down on a bike. We always looked forward to the Goodworth's boy coming although the only "goodies" for Rory and I would be a biscuit.

The boy's name was Ronnie and he was a tall lanky lad who liked to come in and play with our dog, Micky. Eventually, he was called up into the army. When he was demobbed he went to a shop in Welling and ultimately became a shop manager.

I don't know how it was that we had not received our gas masks before we moved. Perhaps we fell through the net when we were evacuated. Anyway, I have a vague recollection of going to Crayford Town Hall where we were each fitted with a gas mask, which came in a brown cardboard box. From then on we were supposed to carry them everywhere we went. The other thing we had to get sorted was that our air raid shelter was full of water. The council sent some men to pump out the water, and line the inside of the shelter with concrete. The lining later formed a support on which bunks rested.

One of our neighbours, William Humble, told us that there was an arrangement whereby he and his wife and child shared our shelter. When this arrangement was made no one realised how long the air-raids were going to last. Sadly, by the time the blitz really started Mrs Humble had died giving birth to a baby, and William and his little boy Eric moved up to the north of England to live with William's mother.

3

School and Church

Our introduction to St. Joseph's Primary school, which was next door to St. Mary of the Crays church, was delayed because we both had German Measles. It was a very small school with a roll of under of a hundred. The long stone building was divided into three classrooms by wooden and glass partitions. There were two classes in every room and every room had a real fire. Mrs Norah O'Shea was the headmistress, and the two assistant teachers were Miss Brewer, and from 1940, a Mrs McDonald.

Mrs O'Shea was an Irish widow. She was a terror with the cane as many teachers were in those days, but the school had a good reputation academically. The only facilities that St. Joseph's had were some outdoor toilets that were in a pretty poor condition and a sink with a cold water tap! The playground was very small, the boys being separated from the girls.

The school air-raid shelter was in the presbytery garden, and when the siren went off we all traipsed across the garden carrying our gas masks. This did not happen very often, but when it did we would practice putting on the gas masks and reading with them on. The priests would come in and try to make us laugh by telling jokes.

I was put in Miss Brewer's class and Rory was in Mrs O'Shea's. We had both always done well at school but my arithmetic was a bit behind. I had never done "problems" and it took me some time to fathom out how to do them. I was then moved up into Mrs O'Shea's with Rory.

Meanwhile, Mrs McDonald had left and was replaced by a Miss Moan. She was given the task of taking the top class for P.E. or "drill" as we called it. One morning a rumour went round that we were going to do somersaults in the playground and that the girls were required to wear shorts. Many of the girls turned up in the afternoon wearing an assortment of shorts, some even wearing their brother's trousers. Mrs O'Shea caned them all with the exception of one girl who wore a floral divided skirt.

When Rory was ten he sat for the scholarship with three other pupils. For the boys it was for a place at Dartford Grammar School. For the girls it was a place at St. Joseph's Convent, Abbeywood, which was several miles away on Bostall Heath, between Erith and Plumstead. Rory and one of the girls passed. The other boy who failed went to the Grammar School as a fee paying pupil.

Mrs O'Shea retired the year that Rory left St. Joseph's after 27 years as headmistress. Sadly she suffered a stroke the following year and died.

When Rory received the news that he had passed the scholarship he was in bed with Scarlet Fever. Dr John Cremin had been bombed out of his practice in London and took over the practice of another Irish doctor who had died. He was in partnership with his brother, Maurice Cremin. It was said that John was the cleverer of the two but Maurice had a better bedside manner. My parents got on well with Dr John and I must say he was always very kind to me. Sadly neither doctor lived to be old. Doctors in those days were on call 24 hours a day and that may have contributed to their early deaths.

When we moved to Barnehurst, there were three priests running the parish of St. Mary of the Crays. Fr. King was parish priest and Frs. Duffy and O'Grady were curates. The previous parish priest, Fr. Malone, had built three temporary

Churches to be served from Crayford. They were St. Thomas More at Bostall Park, St. John Vianney at Bexleyheath, and St. John Fisher at Old Bexley.

Shortly before we arrived, St. Thomas More church was given its own Parish Priest. In those days the curates did not have cars so they travelled around on bikes. Fr. King had a car but I doubt if many parish priests had that luxury.

The Priest in charge of Barnehurst was Fr. James Duffy, a young Irishman on loan. That meant that after a pre-arranged time he had to return to his diocese in Ireland. From the very beginning he was a frequent visitor to our house. Never a week went by without him paying us a visit and most weeks it would be more than one visit. This was partly because we always made him welcome. The kettle would always be on for a cup of tea and if he had any worries of troubles he would always find a sympathetic ear in 33 Inglewood. My parents were not Irish but they were of Irish descent and knew all about the recent history of Ireland. Fr. Duffy could talk quite openly about what was known as "the troubles" and to a certain extent my father was involved in them, only on this side of the Irish Sea. I think he belonged in the Irish Self Determination League.

We had a very long garden in Inglewood Road but because the house had been unoccupied for so long it was very overgrown. I doubt if the previous tenants had looked after it, although neighbours told us that it had once been one of the best gardens in the road.

Even as early as 1939 the Government was urging us to "dig for victory". All over the country public parks, football pitches, sea front promenades, railway embankments, and any piece of land that could be used for cultivation was dug up and turned into allotments. It goes without saying that we all had to dig up at least part of our gardens to help feed the population of the British Isles.

Because of the severe winter of 1940 the potato crop had failed so we were encouraged to plant seed potatoes. Our father was working long hours in the Arsenal so he did not have much time for gardening.

Fr. Duffy was the son of a farmer, so he set to and dug up all the garden with the exception of a little plot at the end where we had four apple and two cherry trees. There was a path down the middle and on the right had side he planted potatoes and on the left hand side my father planted salad stuff like lettuce, radishes, beetroot, tomatoes etc. Sometimes Fr. Duffy would take Rory up to London for the day, and he trained him to be an altar server with two other boys from his class.

In those days, long before Vatican II, there was a lot more to being an altar server than there is today. Perhaps the hardest thing was learning to answer the priest in Latin. Also there was a ritual of carrying the book from the Epistle side to the gospel side, and at a certain point closing the gates of the altar rails. The congregation received Holy Communion kneeling at the altar rails and the altar server would hold the golden or silver paten under their chin.

Rory had always said that he wanted to be a priest and I have two letters that he wrote when he was only nine or ten years old expressing that wish to a Franciscan magazine. I suppose that was one reason why the priests and the Bishop took an interest in him. In spite of this he was very much a normal boy.

Our garden backed on to a large area of woodland that had been the garden of a large house named Oakwood. Part of the ground was owned or rented by a family in Oakwood Drive and their son Douglas was allowed to have his friends in the part of the ground at the bottom of our garden, where they built camps and did the things that young boys normally do. One of the group was a boy named Philip who lived next door but one to us and whose mother held the key to our house when it was empty. Philip was a year younger than Rory so it was natural that they should be friends. He had to ask Douglas if Rory could join their group. As a great concession,

Douglas, who enjoyed lording it over the boys, gave his permission but girls were not allowed. I had always played with Rory's friends in Forest Gate but I soon found two friends of my own who lived near the end of the road. Their names were Pamela and Brian and they were next door neighbours. Rory was also interested in Meccano and aeroplanes. He seemed to be able to identify them all whether English or German. As well as being clever he was also very good at art. This had shown itself very early when he drew a book of Donald Ducks.

So far I have written very little about the War. That is because the first few months that we spent in Barnehurst seemed relatively uneventful. I can remember the excitement of having relatives from East Ham to visit us and showing them round our "new" house and garden and the park at the top of the road, as well as having two of our aunties meet us from school, and spending hours at the swing park with little Eric from next door. We did have the occasional air-raid but as far as we knew nothing happened.

Elsewhere, it was a different picture. The German troops were making their way across Europe and Scandinavia until Germany occupied all those countries. On the other side of the English Channel, in France, the Germans were building up an invasion force called "Operation Sealion".

Going back to 1939, from 27th April British men between 20 and 22 became liable for conscription. At the outbreak of war, on 3 September 1939, all men between the ages of 18 and 41 were liable to be called up.

During the early days of the War, our losses at sea were alarming. On 14th October, U-47 sank the Royal Oak with the loss of 810 men, while in January 1940, the British submarines Seahorse, Undine and Starfish were also sunk by U-boats, as well as the Destroyer Exmouth, which was torpedoed by U-22 with all hands lost. It was a similar story up until the time of the Dunkirk Evacuation at the end of

May. On Thursday 30th May, Mussolini told Hitler that he intended to enter the War.

By 4 June, nearly 200,000 British, and 140,000 French, soldiers had been evacuated, in what has been called the "miracle of Dunkirk." The Admiralty lost 5 destroyers, 24 small warships, and a total of 226 craft were lost altogether.

On that day, Winston Churchill made his famous speech to Parliament, in which he said "We shall fight on the beaches, we shall fight on the landing grounds, we shall fight in the fields and in the streets, we shall fight in the hills; we shall never surrender."

Luftwaffe air raids along many parts of the south coast of England began in July 1940. I well remember the first time the siren sounded in Barnehurst. It was about 5 o'clock in the evening and I was playing on my little bike outside number 25 Inglewood Road. Running home we went down the garden to our shelter, only to find it already occupied not only by the Humbles but also by the Boltons, who lived across the road and happened to be visiting the Humbles. With three of us (Mother, Rory and me), two or three Humbles and two Boltons, there were at least seven people squeezed into the shelter. Fortunately, the raid did not last long and nothing happened, or that is what we thought. I have read since that during these early raids when we thought nothing was happening, bombs were being dropped on Biggin Hill. On Thursday 6th July, bombs were dropped on many parts of the South East Coast. On Monday 10th June, Italy declared war on France and Britain.

I also remember exactly where I was when we heard this news. After school, I had gone to Bexleyheath with my mother to buy tobacco (she used to make Father's cigarettes). The type of tobacco that Father liked was only available at a kiosk in the Broadway, and it was the lady selling the tobacco who broke the news. At the time it was thought to be devastating news, but the Italians proved to be hopeless fighters and had a reputation for running away.

On May 31st 1940, the following article appeared in the Daily Express: "It may be necessary," the Department of Health say "to start during next week the evacuation of school children from some of the evacuation areas, in addition to the nineteen east and south east cost towns which children will leave on Sunday. Mr Malcolm McDonald, Health Minister, in a speech last night said the Government felt this risk of early bombing so real that they must now make as complete as possible the plan for evacuation. He appealed to parents to register their children."

It also said that, "Shelters must be up by June 11th," and "if you have an Anderson shelter and have not yet erected it and covered it with earth you must do so before June 11th, or give a good reason in writing to your local authority. The order was announced last night by the Ministry of Home Security under a new Defence Regulation. Failure to comply with it renders you liable to substantial penalties. If a householder is unable to erect the shelter himself, the local authority may help him if a good reason is given. If not the shelter will be taken away and penalties may be imposed. Covering the shelter properly means covering to a depth of 15 inches on top and 30 inches on sides and back."

Other news included the announcement on 8th July that the Metropolitan Police were to be armed when guarding vulnerable positions.

On Wednesday 19th July more than 100 German bombers raided Britain, while on Saturday 22nd July, the London County Council evacuation scheme was completed with 100,000 children moved to the West Country.

4

War comes to Barnehurst

Shortly before the Blitz started in earnest the sirens sounded one morning while we were out shopping. Running home we made for our shelter, only to find that it was occupied, not by the Humbles this time, but by Mr & Mrs McKinnon. They were the new occupants of the house next door, Eric and his father and grandmother having moved back to the grandmother's house in the north of England. I think it was in Hartlepool or South Shields. The McKinnon's had come from Purley in Surrey. They left behind a nice detached house called *Milngavie.* Nichol, the husband worked at Vickers in Crayford and the journey had become too difficult. When we first met that morning he was reading the Bible. Nancy (his wife) had been a business woman, but had given up her business and was a very capable and efficient housewife. Having no children of their own, she liked me to go into her house and go with her to the shops. Sometimes we would go to Bexleyheath and have a cup of tea and a roll and butter in a little restaurant.

Nichol and Nancy were keen gardeners. When one of the playing fields of Mayplace School, close to Inglewood Road, was given over to allotments they were among the first to be round there digging up the turf and planting an assortment of vegetables. The turfs that were dug up by the allotment tenants themselves were piled up in the corners of the field and children built little houses out of them.

Nancy was our local National Savings representative. She called at the houses of people in the scheme and sold savings stamps that were stuck in books, and when the book was full they were changed for a savings certificate. The money collected went towards the War effort, but participants were free to withdraw this money at will.

While Rory was still at Primary School there was a slogan competition promoting savings. All schools took part and Rory won the prize (a savings certificate) with his slogan "Let us all lend our money for the struggle to be free, for the outcome of that struggle depends on you and me". It was presented to him at a large event at the greyhound stadium. His slogan was on the front of the programme.

The coming of the McKinnon's heralded the end of our peaceful time in Barnehurst. Raids became more frequent and lasted longer, sometimes all night.

The Battle of Britain officially started on 10th July 1940. The German losses were far more than those of the R.A.F. This was surprising given that Germany's great strength was in its supremacy in the air. But in that month, the Luftwaffe lost 165 aircraft to the RAF's 90, while in August they lost 612 planes to 399 for the RAF. This trend continued in September and October, and by the end of that month, the total losses were 1,087 for the RAF and 1,652 for the Luftwaffe.

Meanwhile, in July, the name of the Local Defence Volunteers was changed to the Home Guard, and by then up to 1.5 million men had enrolled.

It is impossible for one to say exactly when certain things happened given that in 1940 I was only 8 years old. What I do remember is this: one Saturday afternoon we were coming home along Woodside Road when the siren sounded and straight away we heard gunfire. Running home to Inglewood Road, we made straight for the shelter where the McKinnon's were already waiting. Nancy always kept a supply of Fox's Glacier Mints there, and she passed them round as we settled down as best we could for the duration of the air-raid. I couldn't stand the sound of the planes so I ended up lying on the floor with my fingers in my ears. For the next few hours all hell was let loose.

Bombs, guns, dog fights: we were surprised when we eventually emerged from the shelter to find our house was still standing. The whole of the northern landscape was enveloped in smoke starting from the Oil Refinery in Dartford, to the heart of London.

Rory who was only ten at the time got out his little bike and set out to look for any damage he could find. At the end of the road he was stopped by a policeman. The Church of England School, (St. Paulinus), had been bombed. Also nearer home, a German plane had come down on the golf course. Some souvenir hunters had been killed when the bombs on the plane exploded. One of those killed was a policeman. Later on Fr. Duffy came round to see if we were alright. He told us that all the stained glass windows in our church and in St. Paulinus church had been blown out.

This was the first of weeks of heavy air raids. Hitler was aiming at invading Britain by mid-August. We spent a few very uncomfortable nights in the shelter with the McKinnons. It was never foreseen that raids would last all night and initially no provision was made for people to lie down. Then something happened that prevented us from using the shelter at night.

One afternoon, in the week following the Saturday when St. Paulinus School was bombed, two taxis drew up outside our house and ten members of our father's family spilled out onto the grass verge. Our grandparent's house had been badly damaged by a landmine, and their first thought was to come to Barnehurst. The rest of the family, uncles, aunts and cousins all thought that by coming to us they would be relatively safe. It was true that Barnehurst was not a densely built up area like East Ham, but nowhere close to London was safe. We only had a three bedroomed house so we had people sleeping in every room. Mrs McKinnon lent us a big box mattress that folded in two. During the day it stood up against the wall and during the night it was on the dining room floor with several children sleeping on it. I cannot remember what we did with the table.

Rory and I thought it was great having our cousins, Kathleen,

Kathleen and Maureen Davies, with Theresa Wootten, in 1941

Maureen and Theresa to play with us, but I doubt if the adults felt the same. Our grandfather in particular pined for his home and the Franciscan Church that was a great part of his life. His house was deemed irreparable and was eventually demolished with a whole row of other houses. Being a builder, Grandpa thought he could have repaired it, but he and our Nanna were obliged to rent a house nearby. I don't think Grandpa ever recovered from the shock and heartbreak of losing the house where he had spent most of his life. The McKinnon's now had the shelter to themselves, but we still used it during the day.

One night everyone had gone to bed except our mother, when from the bathroom window she saw an incendiary bomb fall on Mayplace School which was only a few yards away from the end of our garden. It was quickly followed by another and another and then hundreds of incendiary bombs were falling on the school and elsewhere in Inglewood Road. She woke all the men in the house and they ran up the road with a stirrup pump and buckets of sand and water putting out the fire bombs as they went. Seeing a bomb falling on the roof of a house, they burst into the house and ran up the stairs and waited for the bomb to burn through the ceiling catching it in a dustbin lid that Uncle Bill had grabbed on his way in. The McKinnon's, feeling the heat of the fire, ran up the road to a public shelter with cushions on their heads. By this time everyone in our house was awake except me. I slept through it and missed all the excitement.

After living with us for several weeks, the family decided to rent a house. Fr. Duffy came to their aid and they decided on a nice house, near Barnehurst Station. The only thing our father had against it was that at the bottom of the garden there was a power station that generated electricity for the railway.

In the meantime the air-raids continued by night and day and it was impossible for all of us to use the air raid shelter. I remember being in the dining room with our grandparents when there was a humdinger of a raid going on. In the midst of all the chaos we heard the unmistakeable sound of a plane coming down. We knew it must be quite close and it transpired that it also fell on the golf course, killing the pilot. I think it was said that the plane was a Dornier, a name that has stuck in my memory ever since.

Grandfather, who was still pining for St. Anthony's Church, took this opportunity to point out that Barnehurst was no safer than East Ham. Later that week he and Nanna packed their bags and took their chances in a rented house close to the old one that lay in ruins. Very few people had phones in those days so our only means of communication was by letter.

The other members of the family were having second thoughts about Barnehurst too. Auntie Jill, and cousins Kathleen and Maureen, went to live in Hertfordshire. It wasn't far from London but being to the north, German planes on their way to London did not pass over that county. Aunties Winnie and Theresa were evacuated to Northampton and by all accounts had a miserable time. Fr. Duffy was peeved at the time that they didn't move into the house that he found for them, but he changed his mind when that very house had a direct hit. After the family had gone, the beds were brought downstairs and we lived in the front room, or lounge. Meanwhile, Uncle Bill was called up into the Air Force, while Roy, my father's youngest brother, who would have been about twenty at the time, was called up into the army.

One of my father's friends, a bachelor named Bill Coughlin, lodged with us temporarily while he was waiting to move with the Arsenal to another part of England. He had been a neighbour of our grandparents, and his two sisters, with whom he lived, had moved to Laindon in Essex. Bill was a very shy man, and he was also very nervous. Mother gave him a bed upstairs but he asked if he could sleep downstairs in the hall. He ended up on an airbed in the dining room with us.

I remember until this day the sound of anti-aircraft guns firing through the night and the house shaking when the nearest gun opened fire. There was a permanent gun-site in Perry Street and there were brick-built shelters for the soldiers who manned the guns. Somehow it was reassuring when that gun or guns opened up and you knew they were trying to bring down the German bombers. The reality of it was that, sometimes if the flack was too heavy, the Germans would jettison their bombs and turn round and make it back home. That was why sometimes we would be left wondering what they were aiming at when bombs landed on open ground or housing estates.

One of the worst raids on London took place on Monday 30th December 1940. It is thought that it was intended to precede a New Year invasion. This is what the *Daily Mail* had to say about it on 31st December 1940 in a banner headline:

"Hitler planned Monday swoop. London was to blaze first."

Then the story continued: "Hitler meant to start the second Great Fire of London as the prelude to an invasion. This was the belief in well informed London quarters in London yesterday. The Nazis planned to set big fires burning all over London before midnight. Relays of bombers laden with H.E. [High Explosives] would then have carried out the most destructive raid of the War. The New Year invasion was to have followed. The R.A.F. have given more attention to the invasion ports this past week than for two months or more. Clearly there are sound reasons for supposing that Hitler is still going ahead with invasion plans."

It was the opinion of Commander A.N.G. Firebrace, the London Fire Brigade Chief, that many of that Sunday night's fires in the City of London could have been avoided if fire-watching regulations had been properly observed. "If a proper fire watching staff had been on duty at all the buildings affected nearly all the fires would have been prevented. What is needed is not merely one roof spotter—you want a man on watch on the roof and then a party of half a dozen or so below who can be called upon at once in an emergency. Employees of the various forms should in every case form a rota and stay behind even on Sundays, so as to ensure that their buildings cannot be destroyed by a few small incendiary bombs". The result was that on Monday 20th January 1941, fire watching duty was introduced in the UK.

In Inglewood Road, the men were split up into pairs and a rota arranged so that every day was covered, and when the siren sounded the two men allotted for that night would keep watch for any incendiary bombs that might drop.

My father was paired up with a Mr Steers who lived further up the road on the other side. Although we didn't know it at the time at least two H.E. bombs fell in the garden of a house in Inglewood Road and one of them destroyed an air-raid shelter. I only discovered this when I was exploring the possibility of an unexploded bomb falling in the front garden of a house in Woodside Road. Most of the bombs that fell in Barnehurst were small, but sometimes what was thought to be only a small bomb turned out to be an enormous bomb that didn't explode. It would bury itself in the ground and sometimes lay there unnoticed, perhaps even, in some cases, to the present day.

One such bomb fell in the garden of a house opposite the Manor House. It knocked down the wall and a very long time afterwards the wall was repaired. Years later some workmen digging up the road discovered an enormous bomb that had not exploded and had travelled from the front garden to its final resting place. All the houses in the vicinity were evacuated while the bomb was made safe and carted away to be blown up. This is an extremely dangerous job and it is a very specialised section of the army that tackles it.

In fact, on June 6th 1942, a German bomb that had lain undiscovered for 13 months exploded in an Elephant and Castle house, killing 19 people, and injuring more than 50, while 300 families were made homeless.

This made me think about a house in Woodside Road opposite Mayplace School. We passed that house on the way to school and I remember the wall being down for a very long time after a bad air-raid. Eventually like the wall in Manor Road it was repaired. This played on my mind for years until two unexploded bombs were found in Bexleyheath. I wrote to the Local Studies department, telling them of my concern and they looked up the records and found that no damage was recorded on the house in question. However, a number of bombs fell, starting to impact behind a house in Vickers sports ground, continuing across the road, and then falling in the grounds of Mayplace School, with some finally falling in two gardens in Inglewood Road. No damage was recorded on that house but perhaps it was only the wall that was damaged and therefore it was not recorded.

I remember being in Bexleyheath with my mother on one occasion when a German plane was machine gunning shoppers in the Broadway. We were cowering against a wall in an alley at the back of the Broadway. A bomb was dropped on the "1940 Cleaners" killing at least one of the staff. On another occasion Woolworths was bombed.

Mother never seemed to be frightened by anything. Fr. Duffy was in our house when a very bad air-raid was taking place. He asked Mother what she did when it got too bad and Mother replied "I kneel in the corner and pray." And that was what she did. Our house had been consecrated (by Fr. Duffy) to the Sacred Heart of Jesus. There was a picture of the Sacred Heart hanging over the sideboard and a red light burned in front of it by night and day. In the evening we knelt before it and recited the evening prayer of the Church, Compline.

The mother of one of our curates, Fr. O'Grady was very worried about her son being in danger from bombing. At her request he was moved to a safer place temporarily and another young Irish priest, Fr. Paddy Cox, took his place. Fr. Cox was newly ordained. He came from Co. Kerry but had been educated at Mark Cross, the Junior Seminary, and Wonersh, and was in England permanently, unlike Frs. Duffy and O'Grady, who were only on loan.

To Mother, of course, they were all boys and that was one reason why they were encouraged to visit so regularly. Fr. Cox was a great favourite particularly with the Irish. He was very tall, (like Fr. O'Grady), and had a shock of fair hair. Unlike the serious Fr. Duffy, Paddy Cox was light-hearted, always smiling and joking. He had a good singing voice and on several occasions he brought his music to our house for a sing-song. My Auntie Maggie played the piano and two of his favourites were "Come Back Paddy Reilly to Ballyjamesduff" and "As we sat in the low backed car". Fr. Paddy was one of eleven children and came from a farm in Co. Kerry. His mother was a teacher.

5

Family, Friends and Neighbours

The McKinnon's did not live next door to us for very long. Another house, Number 9 became vacant and they moved into that. As far as I can remember, they were never happy being the tenants of William Humble. He wanted them to pay for bits and pieces of carpet and a few other things that they did not want.

Our new next neighbours, Eva and David McKay bought the house from William Humble. They had been living in Shooters Hill where they had a bungalow. I think they moved to Barnehurst because it was further away from London than Shooters Hill and Eva had a brother living in nearby Eversley Avenue. Eva was a delicate person, having bad a serious operation on one of her kidneys. Her elderly mother, who must have been in the eighties, did the housework and Eva spent most of her time sitting with her feet up on the settee. She was always smartly dressed and had her hair permed. Dave was also not well, although for some years after they moved to Barnehurst he had a very good job at the Delta Steel Works at Greenwich. His trouble was a duodenal ulcer. He was allowed extra milk because of his condition and Eva cooked a lot of fish for his rather frugal meals. She always cut the crusts off his sandwiches in case they should aggravate the ulcer.

Unlike the McKinnon's, the McKay's did not use our air-raid shelter. They had an indoor "Morrison" shelter. It was like a very large metal table with metal mesh sides. The base consisted of a steel mattress. Tests showed that such shelters could resist the debris produced by the collapse of two floors above. It was supposed to accommodate two adults and two young children lying down, but it would not save a family if the house received a direct hit. We knew of a family in which seven people were killed, four of them being children and they were in a Morrison shelter.

The McKay's, like the McKinnon's were very kind to me and I spent a lot of time in their house. When Eva's mother moved down to Headcorn, in Kent, my mother would light her fire in the morning and bring in the coal in all weathers. Eva was very proud of Dave's good looks but although he had a very well paid job and was in charge of a large number of men he was not at all intellectual, unlike my father. When he unfortunately had to take early retirement due to ill health, he was totally at a loss what to do. Apparently he had never read a book in his life.

Before he was too ill to work in the garden, Dave cultivated a large vegetable patch and one of the things I remember him growing was a marrow. He nurtured this marrow and I watched it grow day by day. Eventually, he harvested it and gave it to me. I had never tasted marrow in my life and was very disappointed. Mother boiled it, probably because she didn't know what else to do with it. For many years after that, until I was a housewife myself, I would not even look at a marrow, let alone eat one.

At some time during the War, every road was issued with pig bins. We were instructed to put our potato peelings and cabbage leaves in one of these bins and the contents were collected to make swill for the nation's pigs.

As the air-raids continued, smoke screens were introduced on certain roads to make it more difficult for the German pilots to gauge their position. These were like very large oil heaters with a funnel. When lit at night they sent up a thick screen of smoke. Of course they also emitted an awful smell. Every day a team of soldiers came round to refill them and also to clean them.

Throughout the country, in every town and village, public air-raid shelters were built. Some were built into embankments, others were deep holes dug into the ground and others were just brick built, with very thick concrete roofs to withstand debris. Our school shelter was like that and I believe it still stands to this day and is used for storage. The public shelters were all fitted out with rows of bunk beds and people living near them slept in them. Strangely enough, these people were very possessive about their shelters: even though they were built for the general public, they didn't like outsiders using them. This sounds incredible but I remember the hostile atmosphere when occasionally we were out shopping and the siren sounded, and we had to take shelter.

My little friend, Brian, and his parents, slept in a shelter in Mayplace Road, close to the entrance to the golf club. It was one of three built into an embankment.

In London, 76 (79 by some accounts) tube stations were used as air-raid shelters. Initially of course there was no provision made for people who slept in them because, as I have said, before the War no one foresaw that air-raids would last all night. A committee was set up under Lord Horder, George VI's doctor, to examine conditions in the shelters and decide what could be done to improve conditions. Chemical toilets were installed by October 1940, but these were easily knocked over. By the spring of 1941 local councils were authorised to install water borne sanitation in the largest shelters.

No washing facilities were provided, so people going straight to work either had to dash home first or wash at their place of employment. By March 1941 bunks had been installed in most of the 76 tube stations used as shelters for 23,000 people. Stations were policed to see that people did not start sheltering before 4.00pm. At stations that had trains running through them, 2 white lines were painted along the platform, between the wall and the track. Before 7.30pm they had to remain in the space between the first line and the wall. After 7.30pm they could commandeer the space up to the second line and use the passage ways and stairways. For people travelling on the tube it must have been hell.

As I am writing this over the Christmas period, I must include a chapter about how the War affected our Christmases. For generations our father's family all lived in a tight knit community in East Ham, almost in the shadow of West Ham football ground. On Christmas Day the immediate family—uncles, aunts, cousins—would all descend on our grandparent's house for the grand Christmas dinner. Our Nanna came from Lancashire and she knew how to celebrate a good family Christmas.

After the meal the more senior members of the family would retire to the "front room" and play a card game called "Pit". It involved a lot of shouting and I think it was about buying and selling. Those of us who were old enough played "Murder" and the very youngest just invented their own games. Throughout the day various other members of the family, (Uncle Jim and Uncle Charlie), and neighbours would pop in for a drink and a mince pie or perhaps a sandwich. Everything was home-made. I can taste Nanna's sausage rolls to this day.

Before we went home the "Pie" would be brought out and everyone pulled out a present. The Pie was a large box full of presents, each with a name tag attached. It was instead of a Christmas tree, but I believe in 1938 we did have a tree. Somewhere in the crowded living room there would be the crib, a very important part of Christmas. Is that not what it is all about?

For our family in Seymour Road, East Ham, Christmas 1939 must have seemed strange with part of the family missing. Across London and other big cities, it must have been a sad time without the children who had been evacuated.

In Bognor Regis, the Baillies did all they could to make it a happy time for the evacuees, but they must have missed their parents and families. We were fortunate in having both our parents with us, but we didn't have the usual pile of presents. There was a large Christmas tree in the corner by the fireplace, though, and everyone had a present.

That Christmas was bitterly cold. We had a long walk to church for Mass. On Boxing Day we were all banished from the house for the annual pram race. More than that I cannot remember, but for me it was the last Christmas spent in the company of other children, (except Rory of course), for a very long time.

Our mother had never had to cook a Christmas dinner since she had married our Dad, because Christmas was always spent at our grandparent's house. For Christmas 1940, we were given a turkey by our Parish Priest, Fr. King. Rory and I walked round to the presbytery in the dark to collect it so that no one would see us. The poor bird still had its feather on, and it may have had its innards intact as well.

After that Christmas, I guess that our grandmother would have provided us with a chicken, but Dad would still have had to pluck and draw it. Although I would not have said so at the time, Christmas was a lonely time for me, and even more so when Rory went away to Mark Cross, the junior seminary, and had to stay there for the feast of St. John the Evangelist.

If it was lonely for me, what about our grandmother in East Ham? Our grandfather had died during the Blitz and the rest of the family were evacuated. East Ham was not that far in terms of distance from Barnehurst, but it was an awkward journey involving two or even three buses and a ferry. We did try to have a get together before Kathleen and Maureen came back to East Ham to live, so I suppose it was before the end of the War. Everywhere was very drab across the river, with lots of huge bomb sites and all the houses in need of repair. A whole generation still in the forces was absent. We never tried it again. Christmas, as I had known it before the War, had gone forever.

6

The War goes on

The principal way that we were affected by the War was, of course, the air-raids. From September 1940, the monthly casualty figures were published and they were surprisingly high. For that month they comprised 6,954 dead and 10,615 injured, and although the numbers dropped somewhat over succeeding months, to a low point of 789 dead and 1,068 injured in February 1941, they rose again over the next few months.

For the families who had loved ones in the armed forces, their worries did not end until the War finished. Many were fighting abroad on any of several fronts. For the Navy (both Royal and Merchant) they were in constant danger from U-Boats, ships and planes. Many of our ships were sunk. Those in the Air Force took their life in their hands every time they went on a bombing raid.

Some families had several sons in the forces, and some lost them all. In a little church at Hartley there was a memorial to three sons whose parents were parishioners of that Church. Our next door neighbour, Mrs Jones, had two brothers in the army and they both ended up as German prisoners of war. That being so, they were safe, but those who were prisoners of the Japanese were not so fortunate. The Japanese were cruel, and many of their prisoners died. Those who survived were like skeletons at the end of the War.

Most young men between the ages of 18 and 37 were called up into one of the three forces. In December 1941, Winston Churchill introduced a new National Service Bill, including compulsory service for women. Some men were exempt from National Service because they were in work of national importance. That was usually working in munitions factories; others were recruited for the coal mines. They were known as Bevin Boys, after Ernest Bevin, the Minister of Labour and National Service in the wartime coalition government. They were chosen at random, but I only knew one such man. He used to pass out house every day on his way to work at Vickers Armstrongs. He rode what we called "a sit up and beg bike". That is the handlebars were higher than the saddle. At the time we didn't know his name but we knew that he lived in a bungalow at the top of the road with his parents.

Our father worked in Woolwich Arsenal, and when it was bombed, his part of the factory was closed down and the workforce transferred to other parts of the country. After a time he was ordered to re-open the factory and in a very short time he had all the machinery working, with a work force of up to 3,000 personnel, many of them women. Some of them had worked in the Arsenal in the First World War and others were daughters of women who had worked there then.

The work they did was very dangerous—filling detonators with explosives. There were very strict rules to which they had to adhere, but providing they did keep to the rules, they should have been safe.

Tragically, one day there was an explosion and several women were killed. Our father had to identify the bodies and also represent the Crown at the Inquest. This was particularly hard for him, because they were young women, some with children, and he would much rather have been speaking on their behalf.

When our mother's sister, Maggie, came to live with us, she had to work at Vickers in Crayford, where they made guns among other things. Maggie worked a milling machine. The work was not dangerous but it was very dirty and she came home smelling of oil. Having previously worked in a shirt factory, she hated working at Vickers and she found the shift work very hard. When she was on a night shift I would sometimes go down with her on my little bike. When we reached the top of Crayford Hill, I would whizz down, on the pavement, narrowly missing anyone who happened to be on the hill at the same time. It's a miracle that I didn't hit anyone.

Mum, with our two aunties, Elsie and Maggie—and Rory and myself—in the garden

At the crossroads at the bottom of the hill, there were tank traps—large metal drums on the pavement that would be placed across the road in the event of an invasion. Crayford Road was a direct route into London. Auntie Maggie used to tell us of all that went on in the factory and it wasn't just the making of guns—some people would make little brooches of coins, the head of the King in a V, with a little pin on the back. They also made cigarette lighters and other things to sell.

The worst con was forged clothing coupons. I don't think they were made in the factory, but someone must have had a little printing press at home. Although Maggie didn't approve of these things she did purchase a page of clothing coupons. She used them to have a navy blue overcoat made. I went with her when she collected it from the tailors, and we both trembled when she handed over the coupons. They should have been in a book, so the tailor must have smelt a rat, but he didn't say anything. As long as he had his money he wasn't worried. Eventually somebody "blew the gaff" and the police were called to the factory. I don't know what happened to the culprits but I don't think that it was anything too bad.

At mid-day during the week, there was a programme on the wireless called "Workers Playtime". It came from various munitions factories all over the country, and it started off with the announcement "Workers Playtime" and there would be a loud roar from the live audience. It featured all the best comedians and singers, such as Gracie Fields, Vera Lynn, Arthur Askey, Rob Wilton, Max Miller etc. We always listened to it while we had our mid-day meal, as well as the news and the weather forecast.

The people working in munitions factories could not leave, unless they had a very good reason. Auntie Maggie eventually had a nervous breakdown and Dr Cremin fought a long hard fight to get her released even though she was unfit to continue working in the factory. It was a long time before she was able to work at all and then it was only a menial job, cleaning the tables at Joe Lyons' tea rooms.

Food rationing continued throughout the War and although it tended to fluctuate, on the whole the allowances went down rather than up. In May 1940 the butter allowance was reduced from 8oz per person per week to 4oz. Sugar was reduced to 8oz, bacon and ham to 4oz. Meat started at 1/10d was reduced to 1/6d and then 1/- (One Shilling, 5p).

Part of the ration had to be taken in corned beef. If you were on good terms with your butcher you might occasionally get offal or sausages, or even a rabbit. Meat rationing was the one thing that people complained about most. Men who did heavy manual work said that they couldn't work properly on such small rations. The fact is that it was not so very long since lower paid workers never ate meat because they couldn't afford it. My mother experienced that as a young girl. She used to go with her uncle and aunt to Tring for their summer holiday. They lodged with a family and provided their own food. The father of the house was a farm worker and couldn't afford to eat meat. I expect he killed the occasional rabbit or even a few pigeons.

There was another instance that Mother liked to talk about. They shared a house with a family of five, and although the husband did a full day's work they were sometimes short of food. When my grandfather learned of this, he used to take the wife to the local market at packing up time on a Saturday and buy her a joint for their Sunday dinner.

Margarine was rationed and with a combination of butter the allowance was 6oz. Cheese was 8oz and tea 2oz per head per week. Milk allowance was 3 pints per week per person. In March 1941, preserves (jam, marmalade and syrup) were rationed at 8oz per month per person. Strict fuel rationing was introduced on 21st April 1942.

Eggs were restricted, but in June 1942, dried eggs were introduced at one tin every 8 weeks, equivalent to a dozen eggs. Our mother used to make them into a kind of pancake, and that would be the basis of a dinner. Somehow she always managed to produce a dinner every day. There was a fish and chip shop in Barnehurst and I remember queuing up for fish and chips. Civic Restaurants were opened up throughout the country and you could always get a good meal there. Nobody need have gone hungry but it was often a challenge to the ingenuity of the housewife to think up new meals.

Bread was not rationed during the War but it was in the post-war period. I cannot remember it being a problem. There were some things that were not rationed but were just not obtainable. Among these were bananas, oranges, lemons and onions. I believe that the decision to ration onions was part of an attempt to trick the Germans into believing that Britain had developed a powerful new explosive compound derived in part from onions, in the hope that they would waste resources in trying to produce such an explosive themselves. In any case, I remember Mrs McKinnon growing a lot of chives as a substitute.

Whale meat was available "off the ration". We tried it and didn't like it, but Mother used to cook it for our dog, Micky.

She cooked our potato peelings in the water that the whale meat had been cooked in and fed them to our chickens. Sweets became almost unobtainable until they were rationed. Ice cream was also unobtainable but some confectioners made a substitute that I think was made of dried milk. It didn't have much taste and tended to have lumps of ice in it.

Others used their refrigerators to make ice cubes flavoured with cordial. These sold at 1d (one old penny) each and were very popular with the girls from my school. It has been said that the war time diet was very healthy. It certainly restricted the amount of fats and sugar that we ate and I doubt if obesity was the problem that it is today.

When clothes rationing was announced on a Sunday morning, 1st June 1941, it came as a surprise to everyone. It came into effect from that day so there was no chance to "stock up" in preparation. That was what was intended. If the general public had known in advance, the more well off people would have bought up everything and left nothing for the poor. Winston Churchill was against the idea, but Oliver Lyttelton, the President of the Board of Trade, managed to convince him that it was necessary. Supplies of wool and cotton had fallen to 20% of pre-war levels.

Most clothing was made of these materials that were far less hard wearing than the synthetic materials that we use today. Initially 60 coupons per person per year were allocated. This figure was reduced to forty in 1943 but increased to 48 in 1944.

A mans suit required 26 coupons, a shirt 5, vest and pants 8, socks 3, shoes 7, and a tie 1. A separate pair of trousers required 8 and a kilt 6! This pretty well took all of the coupons for one year, but of course he would have needed more than one of each item. A woman's suit or coat took 18 coupons and an unlined Mac 9, a woollen dress 11, a cotton dress 7, blouses and jumpers 5 each, shoes 7, stockings 2, and vest and knickers 3 each.

At first sheets and furnishing fabrics were not rationed, but when it was discovered that housewives were making clothes out of them, they were put on coupons too. For people who started off with a fairly good wardrobe it wasn't too bad initially. I know for a fact that my mother never had many clothes in her wardrobe and Rory and I only ever had what was necessary, as did most children of our acquaintance.

The difficulty arose when in 1943 Rory went to Mark Cross. He was given a long list of clothes that were required, including two suits, an overcoat, several of every item of underwear and shirts. It coincided with me changing schools and I had to have a uniform although the headmistress was very understanding and relaxed the rules as far as she could. Nevertheless I still had to have a tunic (pinafore dress) at least two blouses, thick Lyle stockings, black shoes, a navy blue overcoat and velour or felt hat. A blazer was also on the list, but during the winter a cardigan was acceptable. In the summer there was a regulation cream coloured dress, although that was relaxed somewhat. My mother made me two dresses, one cream and one yellow, and an old girl of the school sold us her blazer. Panama hats were also on the list, but as these were virtually unobtainable, straw hats were accepted. I didn't have a new blazer until towards the end of my time at the school. I bought one out of my pocket money.

Quite early on, someone stole my blouse and I had to make do with one that was in the lost property box. I never did have any more blouses and I had one new tunic in five years. We were supposed to have a navy blue skirt for P.E., but I had to make do with a plaid kilt that was already several years old. Eventually the school replaced the navy blue skirt with a maroon divided skirt and I was the first in my form to have one. Also for P.E. navy blue knickers were an essential. Some girls in my form had older sisters in the school, so they inherited their school uniforms.

I remember Madame Patrick, the headmistress who succeeded Mrs O'Shea as Head of St. Joseph's Primary School asking me why I always wore my uniform to Mass on a Sunday. It was, of course, because I had nothing else.

There was a shortage of paper during the War, and much of the paper used had been recycled. Our school was very frugal with the issue of new exercise books. During our break time we queued up in one of the corridors to

Madame Patrick In the 1960s

collect our new books, but we had to produce the old full one before a new book was issued. A little French nun, Mother St. Joseph was in charge of the books and she carried out her task meticulously. Many of the books published during the War were printed on inferior paper and the hard backs were equally inferior. To this day I still have some such books including Arthur Mee's *Book of Everlasting Things* and *A Thousand Beautiful Things*.

Quite early on in the War, all railings were removed to be smelted down and used for a variety of things—guns, ammunition, planes, ships, tanks. In fact, by the time all the coats of rust and paint had been removed the remaining metal was hardly worth all the trouble. It wasn't just railings that were collected, but any scrap metal. There was a place on the way to Bexleyheath where the smelting took place. Where railings were removed from public places such as parks, gardens and expensive buildings they were left entirely unprotected. I remember the Park Keepers locking the iron gates to Plashet Park every evening and unlocking them again in the morning.

When Rory went away to school he was thirteen and in a very short time he had grown out of all his clothes, including the expensive overcoat. Thereafter we both wore navy blue gabardine raincoats. They were not as warm as an overcoat so we had to wear a jacket or blazer underneath. As one would expect the more ingenious women came up with ideas of how to manage the clothing ration. It was called "make do and mend". Poorer people were used to doing that anyway. Knitting patterns for socks with detachable toes and heels were obtainable, but knitting wool was on coupons.

Mrs McKinnon knitted or crocheted some curtains out of string. There were no charity shops in those days and in our locality there were no second hand shops either. We did have the occasional jumble sale, but I think Mother would have thought it beneath her to attend such events.

Later in the War, Government Surplus Stores sprang up, initially selling surplus uniforms, mainly of civil defence organisations. These were alright for those who didn't mind wearing such clothes. I remember a girl in my class wearing a navy blue overcoat that was an ex-civil defence coat. It was lovely and warm, but there was no disguising what it was. I sent away for a Wren's jacket but when it arrived part of one of the seams was undone. Mother could have repaired it I am sure, but she didn't bother.

Throughout the War, coal was in very short supply. When we moved to Inglewood Road we went months without any coal and 1940 was a very severe winter. I remember having to sieve the coal because a large proportion of it was dust and no good at all. Eventually we went over to burning coalite. It didn't give off a flame but it was just as effective as coal and much cleaner.

When I was at school I think Mother usually only lit the fire when I was coming home, then it only heated one room and the rest of the house was icy cold. Sometimes we would have an oil lamp in the hall and as heat rises and it would heat the upstairs landing.

7

Wartime struggles, and D-Day

We continued to sleep downstairs as long as the air-raids continued although I cannot remember exactly when our father decided it was time to take the beds upstairs again. In the last 6 months of 1942 the monthly average of fatal casualties was 214, but many of these were from coastal towns.

Around this time, Fr. Duffy returned to Ireland and Fr. O'Grady came back to Crayford. Our Parish Priest Fr. King was replaced by Fr. Brendan Byrne, an Irish Priest. I remember him coming into our school for the first time and a boy called John Rogers, on seeing Fr. Byrne through the glass partition said "He's just like Mr McDermott (my Dad)". A lot of people noticed the likeness including a man who saw them sitting side by side on a bench in Bexleyheath and said "I can see you have your brother visiting". Fr. Byrne never said a word.

Throughout the Blitz, we continued to have the occasional social evening in our church hall. Even if there was an air-raid at the time, most people continued to enjoy themselves, although if they wanted to go to the shelter it was only a few yards away.

It was during one such evening that Fr. Cox came into the hall with a tall handsome American soldier, and introduced him to the Callen family. They lived in Barnehurst and had a daughter, Joan who might have been about 18 or 19. The

Yanks had arrived. They had taken over Hall Place, a large Mansion between Crayford and Bexley standing in acres of land.

When we went to war at the beginning of September 1939, it was difficult to see how we could expect to win. The Germans had been re-arming for years because the domination of Europe was on their agenda, but war was not on ours. It was because we had promised to go to the aid of Poland if the Germans invaded that we found ourselves fighting in a war that we never wanted.

In spite of the inequality in manpower and armaments we never for one moment contemplated losing. Even in our darkest hour, with the threat of invasion hanging over our heads, Winston Churchill made some rousing speeches that gave us great encouragement. On the 31st December 1940, the Daily Mail published an account of a visit that Mr Churchill made accompanied by his wife to the ruins of the Guildhall in London, and how afterwards he spent two hours walking through the City, much of which was in ruins. They inspected a deep underground shelter to shouts of "Good Luck" from the crowd. Mr Churchill replied "Good Luck to you".

As they left this shelter, a woman ran forward and asked: "When will the War be over?" Mr Churchill paused, turned to the woman, and said: "When we've beaten 'em".

And so we struggled on. Everything really rested on whether or not the Germans invaded us. If they had, the story would have been a very different one. But, by the grace of God, Hitler hesitated and his moment was lost. Eventually, the tide turned. The Americans entered the War and there was talk of another invasion, this time from our side of the Channel against the beaches of Normandy. On June 19th 1942, Churchill and Roosevelt met to discuss the second front and the atom bomb. Any invasion had to take place from our shores. From the beginning of 1942 American servicemen were shipped across the Atlantic, 250,000 in the first year with many more to follow.

They were all very well prepared for their stay in England, instructed how to behave and very quickly made themselves at home. Most people welcomed them with open arms, and although I was only a child, ten years old in 1942, I remember feeling safe now that the Yanks had arrived.

D-Day was still two years away, so many of the Americans had time to form relationships with English families, not to mention the girls. They seemed to have an unending supply of sweets for the children, and all sorts of things that we had been unable to obtain since the outbreak of war.

The young man whom Fr. Cox brought into the hall that night was Rudie. As far as I know, the only Americans in our locality were those based at Hall Place, but they were typical of many thousands based all over the country: well paid, well dressed and handsome. It was not surprising that our "boys" didn't welcome them like the rest of their countrymen. Our forces were very badly paid and less smartly dressed than the Yanks. What girl would go out with a poor Tommy who could barely afford a ticket to the cinema, when they could go with an American who could shower then with silk stockings and candies as well as presents for their whole family?

At some time during those middle years, our father joined the Civil Defence. I do not know whether he volunteered or whether he was obliged to enlist, but given the terribly responsible job that he had I would have thought that he was "doing his bit" towards the War effort.

The Civil Defence Depot was at the top of our road, a brick building on the outskirts of Martens Grove Park. The men wore a navy blue uniform with a beret. It was something like the battledress of the army. Their equipment was an open topped lorry with an assortment of shovels, pick-axes and blankets. Their job was to dig people out of the rubble when a house was bombed. In the light of what happened shortly after D-Day, this equipment was totally inadequate, but then nobody knew what was waiting for us round the corner.

For some time there had been talk of "Hitler's Secret Weapon". Nobody knew what it was (except a few people, like my father). We couldn't think of anything worse than the planes that had dropped bombs on us. It had to be something coming from the sky. In the end it was almost a joke because if he had it, why didn't he use it? As the time drew near for D-Day we all knew that it was coming but not exactly when.

I remember sitting on a stile close to the A2 watching convoys of lorries full of soldiers heading for the coast, waving to us as they went by in the run up to D-Day. Tuesday 6th June was the great day. Before dawn, Allied paratroops and gliders began landing behind German lines in Northern France. Allies landed along the French coast from Cherbourg to Le Havre. By nightfall 156,000 troops had landed. The following twelve months were a stressful time for families who had sons fighting their way across Europe.

At Number 19 Inglewood Road, the Bluett family had a son, John, who was one of the first to parachute into Normandy. He lost a leg and an eye. Of course he was the local hero. Many years later, when I was married and had children, his father told me how it had ruined his life. By that time John had lost his wife of 25 years and had gone home to live with his ailing parents. He was always in pain from shrapnel all over his body and he often had trouble from the stump of his leg. I doubt if many people remembered that he was once the local hero.

Exactly a week after D-Day, we discovered that Hitler really did have a "secret weapon". We had gone upstairs to bed as usual and rather surprisingly the siren sounded. We all came downstairs and sat in the dining room. Father went to the front door to watch for incendiary bombs with Mr Steers. Periodically the heavy artillery would open up, but eventually my mother went back to bed and left me downstairs with Auntie Maggie. It was some hours before Father realised that all the German planes were coming down and causing huge explosions. They were not planes, but flying bombs, the V-1s.

When I knew that they were pilotless, I thought the end of the world had come. If they didn't have pilots, there was no limit to the number that could come over.

The first few days were almost unbearable, but we gradually learned more about the bombs. As long as you could hear the engine you were safe. It was when the engine cut out that the bomb dropped, sometimes straight away, or sometimes it would glide for miles before falling on its unsuspecting victims. Also they kept to certain routes until they dropped. One of those routes went right over our house but most of them were to the south and one route was to the north.

Several days after the first flying bombs dropped I was on the way to Mass with my mother when she told me that we were going to the funeral of seven members of the Ilott family. They had children in every class of the school. There were eleven children in all; two of them were in my class. A flying bomb fell on their house on that first night, killing father, mother, three girls and two infant boys. Patrick, Victor, John, Harold and Michael Ilott all survived. The oldest son, James was stopped boarding a ship to cross the Channel with the invasion force and told the terrible news. There were 7 coffins in the church that day, a small white one for the baby: an experience never to be forgotten by those present.

The coffin of the oldest girl, who was about 18, was carried by American soldiers. I believe one of them was Rudie. We all walked across to the cemetery in St. Paulinus churchyard and the family and friends of the Ilotts joined hands around the grave. The five boys were still in Hospital, probably still coming to terms with the fact that their parents, sisters and baby brothers were all dead. Colleen had been in my class at St. Joseph's school and she used to say that my Dad was her dad's best friend. Little Dorothy used to run up to my mother as she went into Church—they were such a lovely happy family.

Soon after the death of the Ilotts, a flying bomb fell on Crayford High Street, killing a lot of people who were queuing to arrange for evacuation. It was surprising how soon we resigned ourselves to the situation. During the day we went out with friends, relying on the fact that we would know if a bomb was coming our way, and as long as we could hear it we were safe. One afternoon I was with my friend Christine down by the river that ran through the grounds of Hall Place. The siren sounded and we decided to come home. Before we had gone very far, we heard the sound of a bomb coming and then it cut out. There was a pillbox nearby and Christine and I rushed inside and waited for the bang. When we came out again, the plume of smoke made by the bomb was coming from the direction of our homes. Running all the way we discovered that the V-1 had fallen on the tennis courts next to the Manor House, narrowly missing a row of houses. Christine lived in a bungalow behind those houses in Woodside Close. The ceiling of her dining room had come down, but everyone was safe.

Another time I was in my bedroom, and looking out of the window I saw a V-1 heading for our house. It stayed in the air long enough to cross the houses in Inglewood Road and Mayplace Road landing in front of the Golf Club, quite close to the tennis courts down the road where the other bomb fell. This confirms my statement that some bombs did actually go right over our house, but thank God none of them fell on us.

The nights were the worst time for me because Mother refused to get out of bed. Not wanting to be downstairs alone, I lay trembling in my bed, while Father was up at the Civil Defence post. One night a bomb fell on the bus depot and Father had to go round to all the nearby houses to see if there were any casualties. Fortunately, all the people were in their air-raid shelters but if they hadn't been they would have been cut to pieces by the flying glass from their windows. For once, Father put his foot down. We were all to sleep in the shelter from now on. He hurriedly got the council to deliver two bunks so that he and Rory could sleep on them, while Mother, Auntie Maggie, and myself slept on a mattress on the floor.

When I said that my first reaction to the flying bombs was that they could go on for ever, in a sense that was true—except that Hitler had left it too late. If the V-1 had been ready for use when we first heard that there was a secret weapon, it would have made a big impact on the way the War was going. As it was, at its height 150 bombs a day were raining down on the Capital, and by mid-September 2,622 V-1's had fallen on Kent, 866 on Sussex, 512 on Essex, and 295 on Surrey.

But by the time they started, we were already in Normandy, and as our army made its way across France, the Germans had to abandon the launching pads from which the V-1's were sent. By the time we returned to school in September the worst of the V-1 attacks were over. I do not remember ever having to go to the shelters in school time after that.

Sadly, the Germans had an even deadlier weapon up their sleeve. There were a few isolated explosions for which there was no explanation. They were attributed to gas mains or plane crashes but as the numbers increased the public became sceptical. They were in fact rockets or V-2's. It wasn't until 10th November that Winston Churchill finally admitted to Parliament that for the last few weeks the enemy had been using his new weapon—the long range rocket—against us.

I heard about it in the Post Office. My parents had decided not to tell me although it was inevitable that I would find out. One of the problems with V-2 rockets was that there was no advance warning of an attack. Once launched, a V-2 travelled at supersonic speed to its unsuspecting target.

When I wrote about the inadequacy of the equipment available to the Civil Defence, this was the situation well before the V-1 and V-2 attacks. The tremendous damage done by each one of these bombs only confirmed what I have already said. Fortunately, there were thousands of American troops still in our country and they lost no time in coming to the rescue. They had all the equipment required for digging people out of rubble and foam for putting out the fires that often broke out due to ruptured gas mains. Not only that, they provided hot drinks and food for the rescue workers and anyone else who needed it.

It was said that when they were aware that a V-1 was coming in their direction they would get into their lorries and follow it, so that when the engine cut out, they were virtually on the spot. Whether or not they had been pre-warned about the secret weapons and were trained up to know what to do I do not know. There is no doubt that our Ministry of Defence knew all about them, probably from photos taken by reconnaissance planes and information passed on from our spies. The V-2's, unlike the V-1's, did not need special underground launching ramps. They were launched from the back of mobile launch platforms, and came mainly I believe from Holland.

One rocket falling on Farringdon Market on 9th March 1945 killed over 300 people in an instant. This was less than a month before the last bomb fell and two months before the end of the War. In this short reign of terror, 1,115 V-2s fell on Britain mainly on London, killing 2,800 people and injuring 6,500. The V-1's killed 5,500 civilians.

The War in Europe finally finished on 8th May 1945, my 13th birthday. There was great rejoicing up and down the country when peace was declared. Every house had a Union Jack varying in size: we had a large ship's flag. And of course there were street parties, although food was in very short supply. I think that from before the end of the War, housewives had been saving for the great day, such things as dried fruits for cakes and jelly, and tinned food for the sandwiches.

An effigy of Hitler was burnt right outside our house. Evil as he was, I didn't agree with that and I am sure my parents didn't either, but it was out of their hands. There was a fancy dress competition and the two little boys who lived next door to us, Peter and Michael went as Bevin boys. One middle aged lady dressed as a school girl in gym-slip and blouse and to my mind made a complete spectacle of herself. On 8th May, my birthday, my friend Pamela and I spent most of the day at a fun-fair in Crayford. Shortly before she died quite suddenly a few years ago, Pamela paid me a visit on my birthday and brought me a plant. It was she who jogged my memory about what we did on V.E. ("Victory in Europe") day.

When all the celebrations were over there was a massive clear up. Parts of London and other big cities had been razed to the ground. All the houses that remained in such districts were badly damaged and had to be repaired. Even in Barnehurst, where there were not so many bombs, the Council went systematically through every road replacing ceilings and broken windows and repairing any other damage. When they reached our house, they replaced the upstairs ceilings which were perfectly good, but by then someone must have alerted the Council to the fact that a lot of the work they were doing was unnecessary. The downstairs ceilings were badly cracked but instead of replacing them, the workmen just filled in the cracks. Many of the walls were painted in orange distemper, not a colour that anyone would choose, but it lasted a long time.

We were suffering from the aftermath of the War, but it was nothing compared with what was going on the other side of the Channel. People were starving and dying of hunger. Germany and Holland were particularly hard hit. Parties of Dutch children were brought to our country, to build them up and then boarded out with families for a holiday.

For some unknown reason there was difficulty in finding homes for them in our locality. My parents did not volunteer to take on a child, but Fr. O'Grady asked them, and they didn't like to refuse. We were allocated two twelve year old boys, Josef (Jopie) and Cornelis (Con) who came from

Enschade, close to the German border. They both came from large families, but they were not poor. Jopie was blonde, and all his brothers were blonde. Con was dark but we didn't see any photos of his family. Jopie came a week before Con and he was very quiet and tight-lipped. He spoke very little English and we understood why the organisers liked to keep the boys in pairs. The first morning after his arrival, he ate some breakfast and then my mother handed him over to me. What on earth she expected me to do with him I do not know. I decided to take him for a walk, but I felt so sorry for him. We reached the front gate and who should be coming along the road but my friend Brian. We had spent a lot of time together, particularly towards the end of the War when a lot of his friends were evacuated. Brian summed up the situation in seconds. He was a real boy's boy and he and Jopie hit it off straight away. Language was no barrier and thanks to Brian the two boys had a very happy time in Barnehurst. We got hold of two extra bikes and took the boys to all our old haunts.

One thing that I remember doing would have given my mother a heart attack if she had known. In some woods close to the A2 arterial road there was a shooting tower. Men used to climb up it by way of a metal ladder, and right at the top was what appeared to be a water tank from which they would shoot game birds. We all climbed up the ladder but the centre of the tank had rotted away so there was just a narrow strip of metal round the edges on which to stand. If we had fallen through, it would have been a very long time before anyone found us, because it was not a place frequented by many people.

Rory had a Meccano set that the boys liked to play with. When they went home we tucked it into Jopie's luggage, also a glove puppet in the form of a monkey that they had a lot of fun with. I must admit that Jopie was our favourite. Con was very bossy, but Jopie took it all in his stride and never appeared to notice that he was being ordered around. He showed great wisdom for such a young boy.

When the boys returned to Holland Jopie's mother wrote and thanked us for looking after him and sending him home in good condition. She particularly mentioned his best suit. Apparently she was concerned about him taking it, probably because it had to be passed onto his younger brothers. It was a typical Dutch boy's suit with baggy trousers. Jopie only wore it on Sundays, but the Canadian Red Cross donated a lot of clothes to the Dutch children. Jopie had a lot of hand knitted sweaters, all beautifully darned by his older sisters. The darning matched the pattern of the knitting. His sisters did not go out to work: they stayed at home and helped their mother with her large family. Soon after Jopie arrived home his mother gave birth to another baby, and they named her Mary.

It is strange to think that Jopie and Con are now in their seventies and probably grandparents. Brian also is much the same age. He married a local girl long before I married David and he had just one daughter. David and I had four

David in the Courtyard at Aylesford Priory

children and to date have eight grandchildren. It is for their benefit that I have written this account of what it was like to be a child in the World War II.

It is not intended to be a history. There will be less and less people around who can actually say "I lived through the War and this is what it was like". I know my children find it hard to visualise bombs dropping on Barnehurst. Thank God there weren't too many. Our old house in Forest Gate is still standing, but the houses in East Ham where our grandparents lived have all been replaced by flats.

East Ham is now called Newham and it is said to be one of the poorest London boroughs, but it doesn't look too bad to me. I passed Plashet Park on the way to my cousin George's funeral and I am pleased to say that it was looking good.

As in my first chapter I described the happy times that we spent in Plashet Park, I will finish this part of the book by saying that for the people living in Lincoln Road life is much the same, although I doubt if the children have the freedom that Rory and I had until that fateful day in 1939 when our lives changed forever.

8

On Holiday in Ireland, and the MBE!

The winter of 1947 was one that has gone down in history for its severity. I remember the snow being piled up on the pavements for months. It was followed by an extraordinarily good summer, the year we all went to Ireland, and the only time we ever had a holiday together as a family. An insurance policy had matured and having gone through such a terrible winter, Mother suggested we should have a holiday. Dad wasn't too keen, but said something about going to the south coast. Mother was disgusted. Apparently they had always talked about going to Ireland, particularly because both sides of our family had their roots in that country and Dad had been involved in the fight for independence before he was married. Dad said his reason for not wanting to cross the Irish Sea was because he had a weak stomach. I had never known him have a day's illness in his life so he was voted down on that score and a holiday for six was booked in Bray, Co. Wicklow.

The extra two people were Auntie Maggie (our mother's sister) and her life-long friend Auntie Elsie. At this time clothing was still rationed, so in the days before the holiday, Mother had to wash every item of clothing to be taken with us for the two weeks that we would be away. It was long before the days of washing machines so it was all done in the kitchen sink. By the time everything was ready, Mother was so exhausted that she suggested we went without her and leave her at home for a rest. Of course we wouldn't hear of that, so we set off for Euston Station, with our various cases, in high spirits.

The journey was a nightmare. The train was packed with many Irish people going home, some having to stand all the way. There were no refreshments and the boat journey was even worse. I stood for the whole crossing, but thankfully the sea was calm. As it happened our tickets entitled us to travel first class, but dad was not aware of this. Towards the end of the journey, Mother managed to get a cup of tea, which she shared with me. I was so thirsty that I didn't notice that the milk was off!

After alighting at Dun Laoghaire, we had a short train journey to Bray. It was too early for us to go to the boarding house where we were to stay, so we had a "slap-up" breakfast in a house that advertised "Breakfasts served here".

Eventually we were allowed into the house of Mrs Hennessy, the district nurse, who took in visitors. The rooms were adequate if not luxurious. I shared with the two aunties and slept on a camp bed. Rory shared with mum and dad and we had to walk through their room to reach ours. I cannot remember what the toilet arrangements were, but I guess they were adequate. Having endured seven years of rationing, the food was "out of this world"—enough meat at one serving as Mother would have cooked for the four of us. Not being a very hearty eater, she would save half of her meat to feed the dogs down on the beach.

There were three or four young ladies—factory workers—staying at Mrs Hennessy's, and two children from Dublin who stayed there every year. We were only about five minute walk from the beach, where there was a fun-fair and various other entertainments. At one end of the town was Bray Head, one of the foothills of the Wicklow Mountains. Being of an adventurous nature, I spent a lot of time climbing the rocks, while Rory stayed with mum and dad, as the two aunties went off on their own. All along the sea-front there were hotels with gardens stretching down to the beach. I wished we could have stayed in a hotel!

Also staying in Bray, but somewhere outside the town, was another family from Barnehurst, named Greenhall. Mrs Greenhall, like our mother was always at the nine o'clock Mass at St. Mary's Church, and, as there were so few people there, they grew to know each other quite well. Kathleen Greenhall and her husband, Dick, had one child, Maureen, who in 1947 would have been about eleven or twelve. Being an only child, nothing was too good for Maureen. Having failed the scholarship for St. Joseph's Convent, they paid for her to go to Stonyhurst, a private school run by the S.U.S.C. nuns in Bexleyheath. In those days, children would wear their school uniforms at weekends, and there wasn't a prouder mother in Barnehurst than Kathleen Greenhall when she walked to Mass on Sunday with Maureen clad in her navy-blue and gold uniform.

Part of the fun-fair was a lotto or bingo table. Being so close to the fair we could hear the players shouting from our bedroom. We could also hear the dodgems, the noisiest thing at the fair. Perhaps the biggest attraction was the "Globe of Death". It was a globe made of metal struts, and inside, two motor cyclists, a middle-aged woman and a young man, criss-crossed the globe, narrowly missing each other every time. It was so dangerous, that they couldn't be insured, so a special collection was made after each performance to compensate for this. At the end of the first week of our holiday we walked down to the beach as usual to find the fun-fair had vanished overnight. It was as if it had never existed.

Everything was still in short supply in England and there were so many things we would have liked to take back with us. Of course we were very limited, not only financially, but also by the regulations imposed by the Irish Government. As one shop-keeper put it, "the country would be fleeced dry if all the visitors bought up all the things not available in England." Mother bought an earthenware mixing bowl, but even that was not really allowed, although the customs officer "turned a blind eye" and let her through. I bought a pair of leather shoes and wore them on the journey home, so no questions were asked.

When Dad booked our tickets, for some reason he could not get the correct sailing tickets for the return journey. He was told to apply to the Harbourmaster's office in Dun Laoghaire. Accordingly, Mum, Dad and Rory made the journey to Dun Laoghaire several times, but all to no avail. They did however strike up a friendship with the great man himself. He told Dad to turn up at the quayside on the day we wanted to return and he would see us alright. A little nervously we joined the long queue for the boat and, true to his word the Harbourmaster came out and ushered us past all the other passengers and onto the boat and into the first-class lounge. We heard a few murmurs from the crowd, but it wasn't as if we were pushing in.

The journey home was more comfortable than the journey out. As soon as we reached 33 Inglewood Road I was banished to the Dean Land Kennels to pick up our dog, Micky. I had taken him there on the day we left for Ireland and when I collected him he was only a shadow of the Micky I knew. Apparently he wouldn't eat and fretted so much that if we hadn't been so far away the kennel owners would have asked us to take him home.

I carried him all the way across Dartford Heath and up Crayford Hill to Barnehurst. When I opened the door of our house, Mother was at the top of the stairs and Micky went into hysterics. Mother cried when she saw him and vowed that she would never leave him again, and she never did.

It may be worth relating that Dick Greenhall, who was a very slight man, came home with net curtains wrapped around his body (under his clothes, of course). One passenger was caught trying to bring home a bale of cloth. When it was confiscated by the Customs man, he said that Cleary's (a big department store) said it would be alright. "Well," said the officer, "they would tell you anything to sell it."

When Mother was telling Fr. O'Grady about our holiday, she said that Bray was too English and she had hoped to see more of the Ireland she had always dreamed about. It was many years later that I booked a coach tour of Ireland for

Mum and Dad in a Killarney jaunting car

Mum and Dad and it took them to the wilds of Connemara and the beauty of Killarney and Glendalough. They enjoyed it so much that they booked another tour and, like the first one they stayed in some of the best hotels in the country—a far cry from Mrs Hennessey in Bray.

It is difficult to understand how a man who left school at the age of fourteen and had no further formal education could climb, in a few years, from the position of detonator examiner to being one of the top men in Woolwich Arsenal. Our father always said that his good luck was due to the War and that after the War he would be demoted back to a more humble position. As it happened, this was not the case and he continued to climb the ladder.

Perhaps he first began to make his mark when the Arsenal was bombed at the beginning of the Blitz and the Filling Factories were transferred to other parts of the country. We had only recently moved to Barnehurst and the last thing our parents wanted was to move again. Fr. Duffy had everyone praying for us, particularly the nurses and doctors in Bexley Hospital. It wasn't long before their prayers were answered and the word came down from above that the Filling Factories were to be repaired and re-opened and full production was to be resumed. As I said earlier in this book, within a few weeks Dad had the factories up and running

again, with a staff of over 3,000 personnel. One would never
know that the quiet man who cycled every day from
Inglewood Road to Woolwich carried such a heavy burden on
his shoulders. His next break was, as he recalled, an answer to
prayer. I cannot say at this stage just what his position was,
but he was working under a man who made his life a misery.
His only chance of escape was, to use his own words, "to pray
himself out of it".

One of his superior's jobs was to submit reports. I cannot
say to whom the reports were sent, but they were obviously
very important; however, it was Dad who wrote them and his
boss got all the credit. For some reason this man was away
from the office for a considerable time, but the reports
continued to be sent, written of course by our dad. After a
time, the recipient of the reports became aware of the absence
of the sender of the reports, but that the reports received were
being written by the same person who had always written
them. Soon after that, Dad's superior was removed and Dad
was moved up another rung of the ladder.

When the War eventually finished in 1945, it was the
beginning of the end for Woolwich Arsenal, but there was
one more job left to do, namely the breaking down of
ammunition. Live ammunition was still in places all over the
world where our army had been involved, and this
ammunition found its way back the Woolwich to be broken
down. I know that Dad played an important role in this, not
physically of course, but he was largely responsible for the
operation and safety of the men who were actually doing this
very dangerous job.

One day, a letter was delivered to 33 Inglewood Road,
from Downing Street. Dad was being offered an M.B.E. He
had always said that he didn't agree with people being
awarded medals for doing the job they were paid to do. When
it came to it he accepted the offer and the four of us, Mum,
Dad, Rory and I, were invited to the investiture at
Buckingham Palace. Dad was given the choice of wearing a

dress-suit or a lounge-suit. Being of a rather portly build he chose the latter. As it was winter time, Mother bought a smart new coat with a fur collar from Smith's Gowns in Bexleyheath. At the time, I was slim enough to wear anything "off the peg" so I went down to Potts department store in Dartford to look for a suit. When the manageress of the ladies department was told of my impending visit to Buckingham Palace, she couldn't do enough for me and a suitable jacket and skirt were found as well as a smart hat.

When the big day arrived, a chauffeur-driven car picked us up from Inglewood Road. Rory travelled up by train from the school at Merrow where he was teaching. We drove in through the gates

Our Family after the MBE Investiture at the Palace

of the palace and through the arch to the courtyard behind the building that is part of the palace visible from the road. Dad was ushered into a side-room to be instructed on the procedure involved in receiving the medal. Mum, Rory and I went into the room where the investiture was to take place. An orchestra was playing in the gallery and we sat and waited quietly with the rest of the families.

At the appointed time, the Queen, (Elizabeth II), entered the room and the recipients of the medals lined up in their appointed place. It was all timed down to the last minute. The Queen was wearing a lime-green dress and the ceremony went exactly as planned. When it came to Dad's turn, her Majesty asked him what he did. He replied that he "managed one of her Majesty's ordnance factories." After that he always had a fatherly affection for the Queen. When it was all over, we went out to the courtyard to await the hire-car to take us to the restaurant near Trafalgar Square.

One of the recipients of a medal was Ludwig Koch, the ornithologist. We had always enjoyed listening to his programmes on the radio, and when Mother saw him outside the palace, she couldn't help running across and shaking his hand. It was the highlight of her day.

We stopped in the Mall to have our photos taken and then went on to Trafalgar Square, where Dad had booked a table in quite a select restaurant, where we had our lunch. After that, Rory made his way to Waterloo Station and we were taken by car back to Inglewood Road. Dad continued to cycle to Woolwich wearing his navy-blue beret from his civil defence uniform and the medal was kept in a drawer, only to be taken out on special occasions to show visitors, who were all very impressed and pleased that Dad's hard work had been recognised.

9

Going to Convent School

When I went to St. Joseph's Convent I dreaded the winter because the school was so cold. The radiators were barely warm, and I always had to wear my blazer. The convent was run by a French order of Nuns, *Les Filles de Jesus* ("The Daughters of Jesus"). It was not, as I understand, primarily a teaching order, but originally, two nuns came across from France with the intention of starting a school for young ladies. They purchased two houses on the site at Abbeywood and the school grew from there. With the industrial towns of Plumstead and Woolwich down the hill in one direction and the smaller town of Erith in the other, there was no shortage of pupils whose parents were willing and able to pay for their daughters' education.

In addition to the two original houses the sisters also bought another house that stood on the corner of Long Lane that housed some classrooms and the domestic science room. They called that house "Ker Anna".

At the time I first went to St. Joseph's, it had already been extended to such an extent that it was difficult to visualise that it had started as two tall old houses. On one side there was a Preparatory School that took pupils up to the age of about seven or eight, although most of the pupils were girls. On the other side was the girls' Grammar School. It was two-form entry, so if we consider that there were about thirty girls to each class this would make the total roll of about 360. This is probably an over estimate because not all the girls stayed on to the sixth form.

Some of the girls in the Grammar School had come up from the "Prep" school and were still paying pupils, unless they had passed the scholarship. In fact, for my first year, my father had to pay the full fee of 4 guineas per term, just as he had to pay for Rory. After that it was free, so the law governing direct grant Grammar Schools must have changed. As well as Christine Hand and myself, another girl from St. Joseph's Primary School, Pamela Sheldrake, started with us. Pamela and I were "best-friends", but she was in Form 1a and Christine and I were in Form 1. Pamela's father had died when she was nine, but he had been a Freemason, and they paid for the private education of Pamela and her brother.

Between the main school building and Ker Anna was a playing field. We played hockey and lacrosse in the winter, but the lacrosse was too dangerous so it was abandoned. We also had a netball court and hard and grass tennis courts. During the summer, two tennis nets were erected on the hockey pitch to give more girls the opportunity to play tennis. At the back of the main building there was a long wooden extension. This housed the science lab and the cold dinner hall, where the girls who took packed lunches ate their meal under the watchful eye of Mother Gertrude, the science teacher.

After my first two years at the Convent we were forbidden to take packed lunches as it was deemed unhealthy. Hot dinners were provided by the school at the cost of 1/- (one shilling) per day or we had the alternative of going in a "crocodile" to a nearby Civic Restaurant. There was also a Civic Restaurant behind the swimming baths at Plumstead, and some girls (myself included on some occasions) chose to go there independently. Other than that I came home, either on my bike or by bus. It says something for the service in those days that I could make the journey home, eat a meal and go all the way back in an hour and a half.

I started at St. Joseph's in September 1943 at the height of the War, when clothes were rationed and the coupons were insufficient to cover essential requirements. The floors in the school were all highly polished and indoor shoes were an essential requirement. I started off wearing plimsolls but when the school doctor saw my feet, she said I must wear a shoe with a heel as I had a tendency to have flat feet. Well, she was right there. I was never able to wear high heeled shoes and to this day I have a dropped arch on my right foot.

Form 1 was at the end of a corridor, next to Form III and was under the care of Mother St. Joseph, the French teacher. I think the only French I ever learned was in her class, but I found it very difficult, unlike my brother who seemed to have a flair for languages and shone at French, Latin and Greek.

Initially I sat at the back of the class next to a girl called Brenda, who, like me, hated every minute of it. She only stayed a short time and I think I would have left if it had not been for the shame I would have felt, although my parents were quite willing to pay for me to go to Storyhurst Convent, a much smaller private school in Bexleyheath. Anyway, I have always been so glad that I did stick it out, because I eventually settled down and had many friends. Never a day passes without my thinking of the good sisters who taught me, not only in the academic subjects, but also as regards an attitude to life and, of course, the Catholic Faith, which has stood me in very good stead.

The first lesson of every day was R.E. with Bible Study for the non-Catholics. On Friday we had Hymn-singing practice or once a month, a sort of Holy Hour in the Chapel, led by Mother St. Hilda, the headmistress. I still think of those Holy Hours and some of the hymns we used to sing. Mother St. James, the history teacher, played the harmonium. She had been a pupil at the Convent with her sister, who was also a nun and she had an LRAM (Licentiate of the Royal Academy of Music). They also had three brothers, who were priests in the Southwark Diocese.

After school on Friday, we had Benediction in the Chapel, which was attended by the Prep school as well as the Grammar School. When it was over, Mother St. Hilda would clap once and we would all stand. Then she would clap again and we would all genuflect, and then she would clap again and we would stand and file out, row by row.

Before every lesson we said a prayer—the "Our Father" and "Hail Mary" in French before our French lesson—the "Hail Mary" in Latin before Latin. On every door in the school the sisters had pinned a picture of St. Joseph. This was to ask him to protect the school from bombs. As it happened, bombs fell all around it, including a rocket just yards away that blew out all the windows. At the end of the War, a statue of St. Joseph was erected in the playing field, looking across to the school. This was in thanksgiving for the school being protected. It very rarely happened that the siren sounded during school-time. We did not have air-raid shelters as such. The cellars beneath the school had been strengthened and on a few occasions we all trooped down the fire-escape to the cellars for the duration of an air-raid.

Returning to my time in Form 1, the Feast of St. Joseph (19th March) was not only the school's patronal feast but also the feast day of our form mistress, Mother St. Joseph. Lessons were more or less abandoned for the day and in the morning a play was put on by some of the girls. The leading light was Yvette Morgan a girl with blonde ringlets who sat in front of me and whom I greatly admired. She had come up from the Prep School and her mother used to have tea with Mother St. Hilda while her father played golf. Her brother was a dental student at Guys and Yvette had riding lessons. To crown it all she had lovely trim ankles and was good at P.E. and games. What more could she want? In spite of all these assets she used to help me with my French, which I found a complete mystery. How could my brother find it so easy?

During that first year, Miss (Mary) Cronin took us for Maths and a Miss Carol taught us English, while Miss

Waterston taught us Geography and P.E. Mother St. James taught us History and Mother Mary Patrick took us for Nature, while Mother Emilia, a French Canadian Sister, taught Art. There again I was absolutely hopeless in spite of the fact that Rory was very gifted in that direction as was my father. Later, Science, Chemistry and Physics, replaced Nature Study. That was, I believe, just a stop-gap subject.

Mother Mary Patrick was the Domestic Science teacher and as far as I know the only Irish nun in the Convent. She had a favourite in our class, Avril Griffin who was a boarder. No-one minded her being a favourite. Avril was a popular girl and later became one of my best friends. Mother Emilia looked after the boarders who slept in a dormitory on the 2nd floor. By all accounts the food they were given was pretty awful and I used to take pieces of home-made cake for Avril to make up for the meagre fare they received.

One of the hardships of that first winter was the cold. The radiators were never more than lukewarm probably due to the shortage of fuel caused by the War. The boilers were tended by an Irishman, Joe, who was also the gardener. He was a great favourite with the girls and loved to talk to us, but the nuns were not too happy about this. ... Joe was one of those Irish men like a big child, not simple, but child-like. He obviously knew his job and looked after the playing field and the tennis courts.

Another favourite with the girls was Mother William, who did the laundry. She had a little building near the back gate and was always ready for a chat. The nuns wore big, white starched coifs and long black habits down to their ankles. Mother St. James told us that they only ever had one habit, so during the summer holidays, they had to take it to pieces and move the panels round so they didn't wear it all out in one place.

There is one thing that has remained a mystery regarding the Daughters of Jesus. The girls or young women who entered that order did so, knowing that it meant practising real poverty. They even used their tooth brushes until they were worn right down and one of the sisters showed us her "black" stockings, which were so old they were green! They embraced poverty just as the followers of St. Francis did, but when, after the Second Vatican Council, the rules were relaxed and a more modern form of dress allowed, theirs was one of the first orders to throw off their habits and veils and replace them with ordinary clothes. Many orders have retained their veils and have some sort of regulation dress that identifies them as a member of a religious order. Ironically, the orders that are having the most vocations are those who still practise real poverty, like Mother Teresa's order and the enclosed orders.

When we returned to school after the first summer holiday, Christine and I were in Form 2, with Miss Cronin as our Form Mistress. Our classroom was on the second floor next to the art room. In place of Mother St. Joseph, we had Miss Robson for French. She had been a pupil at the school and taught us very little French. Her idea was that we should spend our time speaking the language, which is all very well if you know enough to do that. When we had Mother St. Joseph again in Form 3, she was horrified at how little we had learned.

The second year at St. Joseph's Convent was an eventful one because it was the year of the Normandy Invasion. The Mother house of the order was in France, and so naturally the sisters were concerned for their fellow sisters. Soon after the Allied invasion, the flying bombs—the V-1s or doodlebugs—started, and school was suspended until September. A group of us did attempt the journey by bus, but as soon as we alighted at Brampton Road post office the warning went off and some kind people ushered us into their air-raid shelter. When we eventually reached the school we were sent straight home again.

By the time we returned to school in September, the flying bombs were more or less over, but they were followed by something even more deadly, the V-2 rockets. One lunch time we were all in the lunch room eating our sandwiches, when all the windows came in. I am not sure whether we heard the bang, but a V-2 had fallen at the back of the school, demolishing a row of houses. The school windows were broken but fortunately no-one was hurt. I think that was when the rule came in banning cold dinners.

Form III was under Mother Emilia. She had rather a high voice and like all the sisters could be very firm but never unkind. We now had Miss Kerrigan for Maths. She was the official Maths teacher and demanded a very high standard. She was Irish and could be very sarcastic. I got on well with her, but then I never had a problem with Maths. There was a standing joke with Miss Kerrigan, because she could never find the chalk. When it came to Christmas I got a big lump of chalk, put it in a box with a Chad and wrote on it "Wot! No chalk?" I did it up in a parcel and gave it to her for Christmas. She referred to it a long time after with her tongue firmly in cheek.

Every day we had two assemblies in the school hall, one in the morning and one in the afternoon. We all had to line up and wait for the teachers, led by Mother St. Hilda to process onto the stage. We were kept in order by another teacher, and the one that comes to my mind is Miss Kerrigan. In her Irish brogue she would be calling out the names of girls who would be chattering or misbehaving in some way. Nothing escaped her eagle eye. Prayers were said, morning and afternoon and we would all march out to the accompaniment of a pupil playing the piano. The lay teachers attending the assembly wore their gowns.

One teacher that I have not mentioned was Mother Gertrude. She taught science, physics and chemistry and also had a hand in the hymn singing and chapel choir. Mother Gertrude had a very demure appearance and indeed a very precise way of speaking, but no-one ever misbehaved in her lessons. It would be an interesting psychological exercise to work out what it was about the nuns that gave them the authority that some of the lay teachers lacked.

While I was in the third form, one of the boarders died of meningitis. She was the older of two sisters, and I think their home was in Plumstead. On the day of her funeral, Pamela Sheldrake and I were in serious trouble. Pamela was always game for a laugh. She used to tell me the things she used to do when it was her turn to clear up after the school dinners. Initially she had paid for the "shilling-a-day" dinners, but like the boarders' food, they were pretty awful. During the third year, I think, she was going to the Civic Restaurant, but on that particular day she got together with a few friends to take sandwiches for lunch and eat them in the nearby Abbey Woods. I was one of the group—although I knew it was against the rules—but we didn't expect to be found out. Having eaten our sandwiches we walked down to the Abbey ruins and found a swing park where we spent the rest of our dinner hour. None of us had a watch and we relied on the factory hooter to tell us when it was time to return to school.

Well, something went wrong and we were all well and truly late. It would have been alright because our regular teachers were all at the funeral, but Mother Dominic caught us going in the door. Mother Dominic was the deputy head and also taught English. She singled me out as the one who should have known better and said if we couldn't obey the rules, we would have to go. As it happened, on that occasion we were given a second chance. I only knew of one girl who was expelled and that was for nothing worse than hiding in a cupboard during a French lesson. Even in those days we used to hear reports of strange men seen lurking on Bostall Heath, so it was understandable that Mother Dominic should have been so concerned that "her girls" were picnicking in the woods.

Year 4 was perhaps the happiest year at St. Joseph's. Mother St. James, my favourite nun, was our form mistress. She used to come to our classroom after school and chat with the girls who had stayed behind. I once read a brief life of a Dominican priest, Fr. Bede Jarrett. He was described as one who made you feel you were the only person that mattered. That could also be said of Mother St. James.

We had at least two new lay teachers that year, Miss Verny-Boys, who taught French, and Miss Maidwell, who taught English. Initially I was disappointed when I learned that Mother Dominic was no longer taking us for English, but Miss Maidwell was a brilliant teacher. She certainly made a big difference to my English, although that had always been my favourite subject.

Poor Miss Verny-Boys was another matter. She was obviously a very clever woman, but a hopeless teacher of 15 year old girls. It wasn't so much that she was a bad teacher, but she became an article of ridicule. She wore tweed suits and blouses that looked like shirts. Even that wouldn't have mattered: if Miss Kerrigan had dressed like that, she would still have kept us under her thumb, but Miss Verny-Boys was no match for naughty girls hell-bent on making her life a misery. Even the clever ones found themselves drawn into the high-jinks. Word must have reached the ears of Mother St. Hilda and she sat in on one of our lessons. Of course, we were as good as angels.

Miss Verny-Boys lived across the river in Southend, and came all that way on a moped. Before she left the school, she acquired an ancient motor car. That was at a time when few women drove cars, proving that she was quite a go-ahead person. She used to tell us that she lectured in Holland in the holidays and taught adults in the evening after a day of hell in St. Joseph's. It must have been this that kept her sane.

It was in the 4th year that I discovered how many friends I had. I used to meet several of them outside school—Colleen Clarke, Patricia Parr, Mary Hennessey and, of course, Pamela Sheldrake. I was a frequent visitor to the Parr household, but soon after Patricia left St. Joseph's, at the end of the 4th year, and went to train as a florist. I kept in touch with Mary

Hennessey because I used to meet her in the train coming home from work.

I have always regretted not keeping in touch with Avril Griffin. She was a good friend to me during those difficult early days and her own life was not without its troubles. I gathered that her step-father (whose name was Griffin) was killed in the War. Perhaps that was how her mother managed to pay for Avril to be a boarder. Her real father was an Italian named Cromascoli. Avril's mother worked as a waitress living in a rather grotty flat in London during the winter and moving down to the coast for the summer season. Sometimes, Avril had to stay at the convent during the holidays because there was nowhere for her to go.

I only met her once in the City after we left school. She was working for Lloyd's Bank and I was still at the Westminster.

I think it must have been towards the end of the fourth year that Mother St. James dropped a bombshell. With Mother Gertrude she was being sent to run a Convent School in High Wycombe. Apparently, the Bishop of Northampton had asked for two sisters from the order of the Daughters of Jesus and although they could not really be spared, Sisters St. James and Gertrude were the best qualified for the job.

Year Five was the year when we all sat for our school certificate and we were faced with a new, lay, history teacher and no teacher at all for physics and chemistry. Instead we had a retired teacher from Dartford Girls grammar School, who taught us botany. We had to get through the course in time for the exam.

The history teacher, Miss Keegan managed to keep the class in order and was probably a good teacher, but no-one could compete with Mother St. James. The botany teacher, whose name escapes me, encountered the same problem as Miss Verny-Boys. I remember some girls crawling between the benches in the science lab where our lessons were held. However, unlike Miss Verny-Boys, the new teacher fought back. She told us how she had taught for many years at the girls' grammar school where the girls were all well-behaved. She thought that convent girls would be equally good, but she was shocked at what she found. I think she only stayed long enough to see us through the exam. About that time we also had a new art teacher, although Mother Emilia was still teaching some classes. The art room was moved downstairs to the room next to the science lab.

During the fifth year we had to think about our future. Did we aspire to going into the sixth form or did we intend to leave school and go into a bank as most of the school leavers did. At least half of our form chose to leave; among them some of the brightest girls. Miss Kerrigan would only teach Maths in the sixth form to the very brightest girls: my friend Christine Hand was one of these girls. I had no idea what I wanted to do. My decision to go into the Westminster Bank was partly influenced by the shortage of money. Not that my parents wanted any money from me, but there wasn't any to spare, not even for clothes, and taking a holiday job was frowned upon by the school. I would guess that lack of money influenced quite a lot of the girls who left. Mother Dominic was disappointed that I did not return to the school, but I know I made the right decision. About this time, Mother St Hilda died and Mother Dominic took over the Headship.

When I had been working for some time, one of the officials from the Westminster Bank phoned the convent and asked if they could send some girls to work for them. I don't know exactly what was said, but Mother Dominic inferred that it was due to me and the hard work I had done. I was certainly determined to "climb the ladder" and was always one of the first to turn up in the morning and sort out the work for when the rest of the girls arrived. This did not go unnoticed and after about a year I was transferred from the clearing department to the cash department, which was a step up.

I did return to the convent for days of recollection, though, and when I went to Fatima I wrote to Mother Dominic and told her about it. She had my letter printed in the school magazine.

At the time when I was attending St. Joseph's Convent there was always a shortage of nuns to teach. Many of the teachers were lay-women but it could not have been foreseen that the convent itself would be sold and eventually converted into flats. Before that happened, a number of very expensive houses were built on the playing field, and for a time the school buildings and the convent were an annex to Erith College. The school itself amalgamated with St. Mary's College Sidcup where it was known as St. Mary and St. Joseph's Comprehensive School. Even that has now closed and is known as Christ the King Sixth-form College. None of these changes are for the better I fear.

10

My Pilgrimages to Rome

I had left school the year after our Irish holiday and was working at the Westminster Bank in the City of London. In spite of our father's good job at Woolwich Arsenal, money was still very short and with Rory at the Seminary, there was never going to be any money for me. Not that I minded, but I realised that if I wasn't going to be broke for the next five years, my only option was to leave school with half of the girls in my form and get a job in a bank. In all the holidays that I subsequently took and many of them were abroad, I never asked my parents for money and I was very proud of that.

Pope Pius XII had declared 1950 to be a Holy Year. It was a call to as many people as possible, from all over the world, to visit Rome and the four major basilicas—St. Peter's, St. John Lateran, St. Mary Major and St. Paul outside the Walls. Our curate, Fr. Paddy Cox decided to take a pilgrimage from Crayford, arranged by Cox and Kings Travel Agents.

The pilgrims numbered 48 in all plus the Cox and King's two representatives. Only 19 were from Crayford and Bexley parish, 14 were from Ireland (mainly Fr. Cox's relatives, including his mother) and the remaining 4 from places not too far away.

When I booked up to go with Fr. Cox to Rome, he was a little concerned that I might not be able to afford it. Mother assured him that if I said I could pay for it, then I must be sure that I could. The salary from the Westminster Bank was not great, but we were paid seven pounds ten shillings per quarter to cover the cost of our season tickets. With careful management I put that money aside and that paid for the pilgrimage. We had several meetings at the church hall to discuss the pilgrimage, which was to leave Crayford on 26th September and return on the 5th October 1950. Passports and currency had to be obtained and I think Cox and Kings saw to

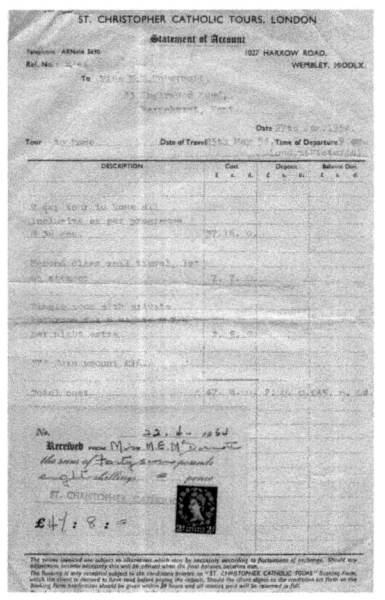

all that. Bearing in mind that the War had only been over for five years, foreign travel was only just beginning to take off again. The ladies in the party were told to take a black mantilla and dress, for the Papal Audience that was to take place on 30th September. Also, arms were to be covered when entering many churches so a black cardigan was recommended.

At last the great day arrived and we all attended Mass at 9:00am in our church, celebrated by Fr. Cox. At 12 o'clock we assembled outside

1954 Rome Pilgrimage bill - £47, 8s

the church, where a coach was waiting to take us to Victoria Station. We were met there by the Cox and King's representatives. At 2:00 p.m., the train left for Folkestone where we boarded the cross-channel ferry.

We arrived at Calais at ten to four, and then boarded the train for Paris Nord station. There we had to disembark and drive across Paris for Paris Lyons station. Then we boarded another train and travelled overnight to Montreux in Switzerland, sleeping in our seats and having excellent meals in the dining car. I remember waking up in Switzerland and breathing in the fresh Swiss air. The scenery was like a film or a picture out of a book—just out of this world. We stayed in a hotel in Montreux, leaving the following morning for Milan, where we changed trains.

During our short stay in Montreux we went across the Lake of Geneva in an open boat to the Château of Chillon about which Lord Byron wrote his famous poem. As it happened, we had studied that poem during my last year at school, so it was all the more meaningful when we were taken on a guided tour of the Château, including the dungeons.

The travelling arrangements on the trains had worked out really well, with the youngest pilgrims all together in the same compartment. Only one person was younger than me: Maureen McCarthy from Bexley. Another young lady from Greenhithe in Kent was perhaps the next in age. Joe Chadwick, who was a leading light in the social life of our parish, was next, and a young married couple, Ron and Kitty Stokes, were on their honeymoon. Perhaps the oldest of our little group was Johnny Mills, a little Geordie man who worked with Joe Chadwick. The journey from Milan to Rome was long and tiring but as we reached the outskirts of the "Eternal City" we all sang the hymn "Full in the panting heart of Rome".

Mary on Pilgrimage In Rome

We were accommodated in a school for boys or young men who were training to be waiters. It was a lovely building, built around a garden, with a beautiful chapel where Fr. Cox said Mass every day. I had a single room with a wash basin in the corner. Downstairs there was a large, well-stocked repository, so we did not have to go outside to buy our souvenirs.

Most days we had to rise at 7:00 a.m. Fr. Cox celebrated Mass in the chapel at 7:30 am, followed by a continental breakfast at 8:15am. We would then be given the itinerary for the day. During the next six days we followed a very full programme, visiting many churches and places of interest, including the four Major Basilicas and the Catacombs. These are some of the places we visited: the Trevi fountain; the Pantheon; the Castel St. Angelo; the Scala Sancta; the Quirinale Palace; Vatican City itself, (museums, galleries, Sistine Chapel); the Catacombs of St. Callistus; the Colosseum; the Church of St. Clement, and other churches; the Mamertine Prison, (St. Peter's prison), as well as many other places.

We were scheduled to have an audience with the Holy Father at St. Peter's basilica, but it was replaced by a Beatification ceremony. The person being beatified was a nun, Maria di Mattias. It was a great moment when Pope Pius XII was carried into the Basilica, most of us seeing him for the first time, and for many it would be the only time. We all stood up, but Fr. Cox, being very tall, apparently was blocking the view of some people. Another priest poked him in the back with an umbrella.

I have been to Rome many times since, but never again have I had such a comprehensive tour. As we went round the city we met many groups of pilgrims, visiting the four major basilicas to fulfil the conditions laid down by the Pope, most of them singing hymns in their own language. The wonderful thing about going to Rome in 1950 was that relatively speaking there was so little traffic. Each time I have been there since, the traffic has notably increased.

Food does not feature very highly in my memories of that first visit to Rome. I think we had a lot of soup and pasta, but on the last day we had some delicious meat. We were trying to persuade the young waiters to tell us what it was, and in the end, they said it was goat. Whether or not that was true, I do not know, but it must have been delicious for me to remember it all these years later.

On the last day, Tuesday 3rd October, we rose at 7:00 a.m. and walked to St. Peter's Basilica for Mass and the closing ceremony of our pilgrimage. At 9 o'clock we had breakfast and at 11:45 a.m., left by coach for the railway station.

Our train left at 12:30 p.m., and we arrived at Turin at 11:45 p.m., going by way of Pisa and Genoa. We stayed in a hotel overnight and the following day, paid a visit to the church where the Holy Shroud is displayed. Unfortunately for us, it was not there, but we did see an exact replica. Taking a walk alone, I came across the River Po, reminding me that this was Don Camillo country. We left Turin at 7:25 p.m. bound for Paris Lyon, where we arrived at ten past nine the next morning.

I have just remembered something that happened on the outward journey and had a happy outcome on the return journey. One of our group (I think it was Ron Stokes) dropped his watch down the toilet and it went straight through to the track below. Luckily, though he was able to retrieve it from a railway worker on his return journey.

On the Thursday morning we had a continental breakfast in Paris and then a few spare hours until we left Paris Nord station at 2:00pm. Maureen McCarthy and I went off on our own and found the Sacré Coeur Basilica. It is a large white building at the top of a very long flight of steps, and it has a large dome. More than that I cannot remember.

We travelled from Paris Nord to Boulogne and crossed the Channel to Folkestone. We arrived back in Victoria Station at 10:00 p.m., a tired, but very happy group of pilgrims. When Fr. Cox died, (at about the age of eighty), his housekeeper told me that he still remembered the time in 1950 when he took a party to Rome. I hope, wherever he is, that Paddy Cox remembers the eighteen year old girl who first acquired a taste for foreign travel on his pilgrimage from Crayford.

When I went to Rome in 1950 I had no idea that Pope Pius XII was just the first of four popes that I would be privileged to see during my life, that is, Pope Pius XII, Pope John XXIII, Pope Paul VI and Pope John Paul II. The second time I went to Rome was in 1954 for the Canonisation of

Pope Pius X. I went with a Pilgrimage organised by St. Christopher Tours who arranged my visit to Fatima. We travelled by train again and stayed in a hotel close to the Basilica of St. Mary Major.

The Canonisation Ceremony was the first one to take place out of doors in St. Peter's Square. There were no seats allocated so quite early in the morning we walked to St. Peter's and took our places as close as we could to the Basilica steps where the ceremony took place in the late afternoon. How I managed to stand there all day I cannot imagine. Apart from the heat and the long wait I cannot remember going to the toilet and was not even aware that there were any toilets close to the square.

Eventually the Cardinals from all over the world came in procession to take their places near the steps, and finally the Pope (Pius XII) was carried to his throne and the ceremony began. It is not surprising that after so many years I cannot remember many details, but the fact is that I was there. When it was all over, we walked back to our hotel for a much-appreciated meal.

Later that evening the glass coffin containing the body of Pope St. Pius X was brought to the Basilica of St. Mary Major. We watched the proceedings from the window of my room in the hotel. The front of the Basilica was lit up by hundreds of small lights.

The one thing I remember about St. Pius X is that he made it possible for children to receive Holy Communion at the age of seven. He also encouraged the frequent reception of Holy Communion. Born of a poor family in Riese (Venetia) in 1835, he died in 1914; he had a reputation for miracles, simplicity and poverty. He wrote in his Will, "I was born poor, I have lived poor and I wish to die poor." Certain aspects of the wealth and ceremonial at the Vatican were profoundly distasteful to him. There was a popular outcry for his canonisation as soon as he died.

I think it was during that visit to Rome that I went to the Pope's summer residence at Castel Gandolfo, where we gathered in the courtyard to receive the blessing of the Pope. Later a large hall was erected to cater for the large number of pilgrims visiting the Castel. Pope Pius XII died in 1958 and was succeeded by Pope John XXIII.

Going up to London every day in the train I had been reading a book called *Have you been to Rome?* It wasn't long before I had itchy feet and started planning my next visit to the Holy City. I decided to go on my own for two weeks, taking in the week before Easter and the week after. I stayed in the same hotel close to the Basilica of St. Mary Major. The man at the desk in the foyer said that he had worked for a number of years in a hotel in Ireland (Co. Wicklow, I believe). Also staying at the hotel was an Irish priest from Co. Mayo. He was a chaplain to N.A.T.O., and had gone to Rome to find the sun (so he said).

A visit to Rome at Easter time is an unforgettable experience for any Catholic, but unfortunately many of the organised pilgrimages do not arrive until Holy Saturday, and very few remain for more than a few days. Any attempt to describe the solemnity and beauty of the Holy Week services would require the genius of a poet, but perhaps a few general comments on my visit to Rome would be of interest.

Early in Holy Week, I paid a visit to the *Scala Sancta* (Holy Stairs). According to tradition these are the original stairs which Christ ascended in the house of Pilate, and were brought to Rome by St. Helena, the mother of Constantine, the first Christian Roman Emperor. They may only be ascended on the knees, and during Holy Week, thousands of pilgrims make the ascent, while meditating on the Passion. The fourth of the great churches of Rome, and the largest dedicated to Our Blessed lady, is the Basilica of St. Mary Major. It was here that I attended the Holy Week ceremonies. At the Veneration of the Cross, the Crucifix was guarded by one of the Palatine Guards, and I saw many of the

Italians kissing, not just the feet but all five wounds of Our Blessed Lord. The crowds receiving Holy Communion was so great that they were controlled by two more guards. During the Vigil, we sat in the darkened Church, illuminated by only the Paschal Candle, and heard the deacon chant, "Lumen Christi!" I thought of the little church at Crayford and indeed of the churches all over the world, where precisely the same words were being sung and the same responses given. Throughout all the ceremonies, the singing was magnificent, and this was one of the reasons why I had made the journey to Rome for Holy Week.

On the morning of Easter Sunday, regardless of the rain, thousands made their way to St. Peter's Square to receive the first Easter Blessing of Pope John XXIII. After the tall, elegant figure of Pope Pius XII, his Holiness looked very small. In spite of the exhilaration which I felt at being present on such an occasion, I could not help feeling sorry for this humble little man who carried the burdens of the world on his shoulders. Unlike the pilgrims of old, who made the long and painful journey to Rome on foot, modern pilgrims arrived by plane, train or motor-coach. Special coaches and guides are hired to take them on tours of the city, and they are rushed from place to place at an alarming pace. This time I was in a position to pity these poor victims of the age of speed, for I was seeing Rome at my leisure.

One morning, on finding the Roman Forum thronged with people of all nationalities; I turned my back on the crowds and ascended the Caelian Hill by way of a quiet country lane. On the side of the road were the Stations of the Cross, and at the top of the hill was a little Franciscan church dedicated to St. Bonaventure. H.V. Morton, the religious author, said of this lane, that it is just the place where one would expect to meet St. Francis. Seated on a step in front of the twelfth Station, an old man was dozing in the sun, and a few yards away lay his dog, a big old Springer Spaniel. Some days later, I peeped through a gate on the other side of the wall, and he was still sitting there, with his faithful old dog stretched out in the same place. Maybe he was a poet, dreaming dreams of ancient Rome.

English Catholics owe their faith to St. Gregory the Great at whose command St. Augustine set out from Rome to bring Christianity to our land. As a young man, Gregory renounced his riches and converted his ancestral home into a monastery where he lived as a monk for many years. The site of that monastery is now occupied by a church dedicated to St. Gregory the Great. It was with a feeling of awe that I stood on the steps overlooking the Via Triumphalis and admired the surroundings which the Apostle of England must have looked upon every day of his monastic life. Across the way was the Palatine, where for centuries, the Emperors of Rome built there palaces, and a few yards down the road was the Forum, where St. Gregory saw the flaxen-haired Angles and likened them to angels.

Well, there are so many other things one could say about Rome, particularly at Easter time. On Good Friday that year I visited as many churches between the Caelian and the Esquiline hills as time would allow. The altars of repose were a glory to behold. From the largest Basilica to the smallest chapel, the array of flowers was unsurpassed by anything I had ever seen in England. While on a visit to St. Peter's, I spent several minutes admiring the wonderful Pieta, carved by the young Michelangelo. He carved his name on the band across Our Lady's chest, so that everyone would know that it was his masterpiece. I also visited the tomb of the late Pope Pius XII. The last time I had seen him alive was three years previously at a mass-audience given at Castel Gandolfo. Even now, I hope and pray that at some future date I may be in Rome again when he is raised to the altars of the Church.

On my return I wrote an article entitled, "The Eternal City", about my visit for a magazine called "The Toddler" that was at that time produced for our parish of St. Mary of the

Crays. I think it is better than anything that I could write now.

My next visit to Rome was a two-centre holiday with Swans. And I was accompanied by my friend Christine and her sister Maureen. We spent a week in Rome and a week in Santa Margherita, a coastal resort.

Our accommodation in Rome was a Pensione overlooking the Square in front of the Railway Station. It was a bit of a "come-down" from the hotel where I had stayed previously and I think we had to provide our own meals. It must have been in the height of summer, because I remember the heat was unbearable. I cannot really remember how we spent our time except that we had to rest in the afternoon because of the heat.

Swans arranged a coach trip to Castel Gandolfo and a mass audience with Pope Paul VI. Maureen and Christine declined to go, but I wanted to see the Pope so I accepted and went along with the coach load of people whom I had never seen before. I got talking to an American lady and our conversation got round to the fairly recently elected President John Kennedy. The recent death of his baby came up and I made some remark about losing a child being a heavy cross to bear. I was quite surprised when the American lady said, "Yes, and the biggest cross she (Jacqui Kennedy) had to bear was being married to him!"

The audience took place in a hall that had recently been erected for that purpose. Our week in Santa Margherita was uneventful. I think we must have stayed in a hotel, but I cannot really remember, surprisingly for me.

On our outward journey we befriended a young couple and a young lady, the friend of the girl. We met the young couple on the return journey, but their friend was not with them. Apparently she had become friends with a young Italian man and had decided to stay with him, even though she did not speak Italian and he did not speak English. They had been given the unenviable task of breaking the news to her parents.

11

My Pilgrimage to Fatima

In our parish of St. Mary of the Crays, it was the custom to celebrate the Feast of Christ the King with a social event. Sometimes, our parishioners would perform a play, and in 1951 we had a film show about the apparitions in Fatima. Very few people would have known about Fatima at that time. I certainly didn't, and I think my parents only had a faint idea of what happened in that remote village in Portugal in 1917.

Briefly, three peasant children, Lucia, Jacinta and her brother Francisco, claimed to have been visited by Our Blessed Lady on a number of occasions. The first visit was on 13th May 1917, and then on the 13th of every month until October, when a miracle was worked in the sight of thousands of people to prove that the claims of the children were genuine.

The film, by today's standards was a very amateurish production, in black and white of course, but it was a true version of what had happened at Fatima thirty-four years before. In those years, nothing much had changed, except the building of the Basilica. Many of the people in the film were actually alive at the time of the apparitions and had witnessed the "miracle of the sun", about which I shall write later. I don't think that at the time I had any idea of visiting Fatima.

although the pilgrimage to Rome had aroused in me a yearning for further travel.

Soon after seeing the film I changed my job. Many of the girls were leaving to go to overseas banks where the pay was better. Initially I said I wouldn't do that because I was happy where I was and had definitely improved my position compared to when I first started working there at the age of sixteen.

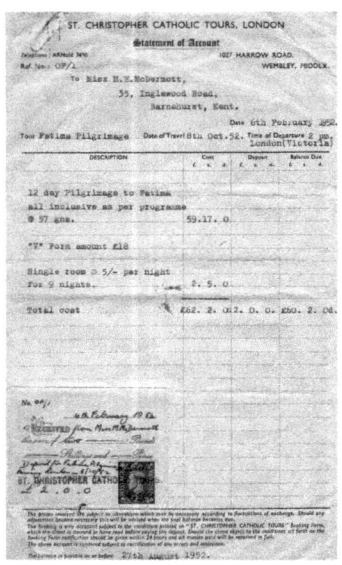

1952 Pilgrimage bill - £62, 2s

However the appeal of more money won in the end and I wrote to the Canadian Bank of Commerce just along the road from the Westminster Bank and asked if they had any vacancies. They took me on for the princely sum of £5 per week, which was £2-5s more than I had been receiving at the Westminster Bank. Also there were bonuses and a monthly food parcel for every employee (from Canada).

Early in 1952 I saw in one of the papers an advert from a Catholic Travel Agency called St. Christopher's Tours. Sending for their brochure, I discovered that the agency had only recently been set up by a Mr de Kerckhove, working from his own home, and doing most of the work himself including acting as a courier.

There was just one pilgrimage to Fatima on the 13th October and with my recent increase in salary I reckoned I could just about save enough money to pay for a place. I had not been looking for a pilgrimage to Fatima, but it was something different and as I had recently seen the film in our church hall, it just seemed like a good idea. Unfortunately I did not keep the itinerary (not surprising after 60 years) so I have to rely on my memory to relate the details. We were going to Fatima for the celebration of the 13th of October so we must have left Victoria Station on the 9th. We travelled as far as Paris, where we spent the night, resuming our journey the following morning. We travelled all that day and overnight from Paris to Lisbon by train, sleeping in our seats, but I think we travelled 1st class. For part of the journey we shared our compartment with the wife of a Portuguese diplomat and her daughter. They had been in England during the War, staying in Westerham in Kent. The mother was at great pains to impress on us that the people, (mainly women), whom we saw working in the fields were not poor. They had everything they needed and just lived a very simple way of life.

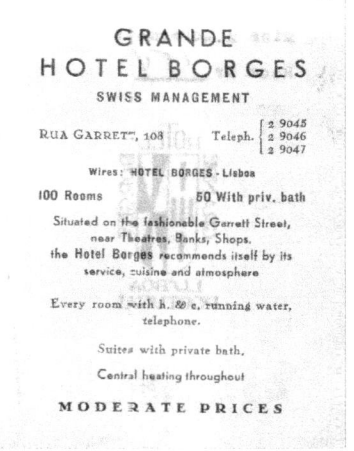

GRANDE
HOTEL BORGES
SWISS MANAGEMENT

RUA GARRETT, 108   Teleph. { 2 9045 / 2 9046 / 2 9047

Wires: HOTEL BORGES - Lisboa

100 Rooms   50 With priv. bath

Situated on the fashionable Garrett Street, near Theatres, Banks, Shops.
the Hotel Borges recommends itself by its service, cuisine and atmosphere

Every room with h. & c. running water, telephone.

Suites with private bath.

Central heating throughout

MODERATE PRICES

Our party was made up of about 30 people. Two of them were priests, both Irish, but one of them was at that time working in England. The other priest was from Co. Longford in Ireland and he was accompanied by a man from his parish named James Lovell. It was James's second visit to Fatima and he was just at the start of a lifelong crusade to promote the message of Fatima to the people of Ireland. He was what I would describe as a typical Irish countryman. His family ran a turf business in Ballymahon. We discovered that we had a friend in common, Fr. O'Grady, who had returned to Ireland from his stint of about ten years in Crayford and was, I believe, the curate at Lanesborough also in Co. Longford. Many years later he returned as parish priest.

James Lovell seemed to spend all his time saying the rosary. He said that so many people had asked him to pray for them and he had to get through so many rosaries. When he wasn't praying he was quite a jolly character. He had a little joke going with me about my great grandfather coming from Roscommon, the neighbouring county to Longford.

I was befriended by an Irish Lady, Mrs Power, who had previously been to Lourdes as a stretcher patient. Having recovered from the TB that had afflicted her, she was making the pilgrimage to Fatima in thanksgiving. There was only one other young person in the party, although I think she was older than myself. She had been more or less forced to book a place on the pilgrimage by her uncle, who was a priest and had paid for her to go. She had obviously made it known that she was there under duress and one of the priests asked me if I would have a word with her. I thought that would do more harm than good. Having spent a restful night in Lisbon after our long train journey, we set off in a coach for Fatima. As we neared the shrine we were passing thousands of people making their way on foot, many of them bare-footed and some even on their knees.

There was no provision made for pilgrims, no food shops or even toilets, just three or four souvenir shops with rooms behind them where the ladies in our party slept. The men went to the Consolata Missionary Seminary that was visible in the distance. We had our meals in a house where an English family lived. Their son was home from his boarding school in England because there had been a fire. Apparently, the previous year, when Mr de Kerckhove had taken a party to Fatima they had slept on the coach and he didn't know until we arrived whether or not we would also be sleeping on the coach. At the end of the little row of souvenir shops there was an outside toilet. We were not told about these difficulties in advance. I am pleased that Mr de Kerckhove was wise enough not to tell us, because if I had known, especially about the lack of toilets, I would have thought twice about going.

The first night in Fatima was a vigil, so we were up all night. In the mists of time, I cannot remember how we spent that night. There were thousands of pilgrims gathered around the shrine, most of them Portuguese, so any organised prayer would have been in that language. I vaguely remember going into the Basilica and seeing the burial place of Francisco and Jacinta. If there were any English people among the crowds I cannot remember seeing them.

On the morning of 13th there was the closing ceremony of pilgrimages for 1952. The statue of Our Lady was carried shoulder high around the Cova da Iria, (the large expanse of ground in front of the Basilica), while hymns were sung and all

Jacinta and Francisco's parents, Manuel and Olimpia Marto (left and centre)

the pilgrims waved their hankies. The statue was then replaced in the little shelter that had been built at the place where the tree stood, over which Our Lady had appeared.

It was very fortunate for us that the young boy was home from his English boarding school, because he was able to take us to all the places of interest, including Valhinos, the place where Our Lady appeared to the children after they had been abducted by the local mayor on 13 August, and also the village where the parents of Francisco and Jacinta were still living. They came out to meet our little party and shook hands with us, and the old lady said a few words to us (in Portuguese of course). She said something about it all happening a long time ago. In fact it was only 35 years, but as well as losing Francisco and Jacinta to the Spanish Flu at the end of the First World War, they also lost other children. Shaking hands with the parents of Francisco and Jacinta was one of the highlights of my pilgrimage. They probably did not live all that long after our visit. They were in fact the parents of two future saints.

On the morning of the 14th October we left Fatima and returned to the hotel in Lisbon. We saw very little of the city itself, so we must have either continued our journey home on the 14th or on the morning of the 15th October. We broke our journey at San Sebastian in Spain, where we spent a couple of days before finally travelling through France and across the English Channel and home.

I have never been to Fatima since, but I was always glad that I made the pilgrimage before it developed into the shrine it is today. Of course it is inevitable that if people are to travel from all over the world to see the place where Our Lady appeared, provision must be made to accommodate them, as has happened at Lourdes.

Many years later, a friend of ours made a pilgrimage to Fatima and on her return told us about a man who had spent his life promoting the message of Fatima to the people of Ireland. She was amazed to learn that I had been on a pilgrimage with James Lovell at the beginning of his crusade. Apparently, before he died he wrote a booklet entitled *An Account of my Stewardship* telling about how it all started and how his crusade developed. Our friend managed to obtain a copy of the booklet that I still treasure.

The supernatural events of Fatima really began in 1915, when three girls, including Lucia dos Santos saw an angel while they were reciting the Rosary. They had been watching their sheep in a rocky olive grove close to Aljustrel, near Fatima. Soon after starting the Rosary, they saw a figure in the air above the trees which looked like a statue made of snow. The children were alarmed but continued praying with their eyes fixed on the figure. When they finished praying, the vision disappeared. Lucia did not tell her parents what they had seen, but the younger children could not keep it to themselves and soon it was all round the village. When questioned by her mother, Lucia said that it looked like a person wrapped up in a sheet.

In 1916, the year before Our Lady appeared to the three children, Lucia, and Jacinta and Francisco Marto, the angel appeared again, this time to the three future seers. Instead of disappearing as the vision had done on the previous occasions it came down closer to the children until they could see that it was a beautiful youth of about 14 or 15 years, whiter than snow and transparent as crystal. He came right down and stood among them and said: "Do not be afraid. I am the angel of peace. Pray with me."

He bent down until his forehead touched the ground and said, "My God, I believe, I adore, I hope and I love you. I ask pardon for those who do not believe, do not adore, do not hope and do not love you." He made the children to repeat these words three times. When he had risen from the ground and before disappearing, he said, "Pray thus. The Hearts of Jesus and Mary are attentive to the voice of your supplications." From then on the children spent much of their time looking after their sheep and repeating the prayers the angel had taught them.

The next time the angel appeared, the children were playing by a well at the bottom of the garden behind Lucia's home. This was one of the places we visited with the English boy. The angel asked the children what they were doing before saying, "Pray, pray very much! The most holy Hearts of Jesus and Mary have designs of mercy on you. Offer prayers and sacrifices constantly to the Most High." Lucia asked "How are we to make sacrifices?" The Angel responded: "Make everything you can a sacrifice and offer it to God as an act of reparation for the sins by which he is offended and in supplication for the conversion of sinners. You will thus draw down peace upon your country. I am its Angel Guardian, the Angel of Portugal. Above all, accept and bear with submission all the sufferings which the Lord will send you."

The final angelic apparition took place one day in the autumn of 1916, after the children had finished their lunch and were praying as the angel had taught them. All at once they were aware of a bright light and raising their heads, they saw the angel standing in front of them. In his left hand he held a chalice. Suspended above the chalice was a sacred host, and from this suspended host drops of blood fell into the chalice. The angel left the chalice suspended in the air, and kneeling down, he prayed, "Most Holy Trinity, Father, Son and Holy Spirit, I adore you profoundly and offer you the most precious Body, Blood, Soul and Divinity of Jesus Christ, present in all the tabernacles of the world, in reparation for the outrages, sacrileges and indifferences with which he himself is offended. And through the infinite merits of his most Sacred Heart and the Immaculate Heart of Mary, I beg of you the conversion of poor sinners."

Three times the children repeated the prayer. The angel then placed the host on Lucia's tongue and shared the precious blood from the chalice between Francisco and Jacinta, saying at the same time, "Take and drink the Body and Blood of Jesus Christ, horribly outraged by ungrateful men! Make reparation for their crimes and console your God." The children remained prostrate, repeating the most Holy Trinity prayer until it was dark.

The day that Our Lady first appeared, 13 May 1917, the children were minding the sheep in a place called the Cova da Iria. Shortly after arriving at the Cova, there was a flash of lightning and the children feared that a storm was on the way. They had gathered the sheep together, when there was another flash like lightning and then, a few steps further on, standing on the top branches of a young holm oak tree, was a beautiful lady, dressed all in white. She was described as being more brilliant than the sun and radiated a light clearer than a crystal glass filled with sparkling water. She told the children not to be afraid, and Lucia in her childish innocence asked where she came from. The reply was, "I am from Heaven". Then Lucia asked, "What do you want of me?"

"I have come to you to come here for six months in succession, on the 13th day at this hour. Later on I will tell you who I am and what I want" The children asked several other questions: Would they go to heaven? Were several of their friends who had died in heaven? The Lady told them that one of their friends was in Purgatory. This was a stark rebuff to our world, especially since some people choose to believe that Purgatory does not exist.

The second apparition, on 13th June, was on the feast of St. Anthony, Portugal's patron saint. As the Lady had promised, she appeared at the same time and in the same place. Lucia asked again the same question she had asked the previous month, "What do you want of me?"

"I want you to come here on the 13th of next month, to pray the rosary every day and to learn to read. Later I will tell you what I want".

Then Lucia said, "I would like to ask you to take us to Heaven." The Lady answered, "Yes, I will take Francisco and Jacinta soon, but you are to stay here for some time longer. Jesus wishes to make use of you to make me known and loved. He wants to establish in the world, devotion to my Immaculate Heart. I promise salvation to those who embrace it and those souls will be loved by God like flowers placed by me to adorn his throne".

"Am I to stay here alone?" asked Lucia.

The Lady replied, "No, my daughter. Are you suffering a great deal? Don't lose heart, I will never forsake you. My Immaculate Heart will be your refuge and the way that will lead you to God."

The third apparition took place on 13th July. By now, three or four thousand people had gathered at the Cova, many of them saying the Rosary and on their knees. Our Lady didn't keep them waiting and again Lucia asked, "What do you want of me?" This time the Lady told them to say the Rosary, but in honour of Our Lady of the Rosary, in order to obtain peace for the world and the end of the War, because, "only she can help you". She also promised to work a miracle so that all would believe, and added, "Sacrifice yourself for sinners and say many times, especially when you make some sacrifice: O Jesus, it is for love of you, for the conversion of sinners, and in reparation for the sins committed against the Immaculate Heart of Mary."

For the third time the lady opened her hands and this time the aspect of eternity the children were shown was hell. Lucia says, "The rays of light seemed to penetrate the earth and we saw, as it were, a sea of fire. Plunged in this fire were demons and souls in human form like transparent burning embers all blackened or burnished bronze floating about in the conflagration, now raised into the air by the flames that issued from within themselves together with great clouds of smoke, now falling back on every side like sparks in huge fires, without weight or equilibrium amid shrieks and groans of pain and despair which horrified us and made us tremble with fear.

"Terrified and as if to plead for succour we looked up at Our Lady, who said to us so kindly and sadly, 'You have seen hell, where the souls of poor sinners go. To save them, God wishes to establish in the world devotion to my Immaculate Heart. If what I say to you is done, many souls will be saved and there will be peace. The War is going to end, but if people do not cease offending God, a worse one will break out during the pontificate of Pius XI. When you see a night illuminated by an unknown light, know that this is the great sign given you by God that he is about to punish the world for its crimes by means of war, famines and persecutions of the Church and of the Holy Father' ".

The children were instructed that all of this was to remain a secret, but once it was known the Lady had given them a secret, they were besieged by people anxious to find out its contents. The children also saw a vision of a Bishop dressed in white, which was not revealed until the year 2,000, but the first two parts of the secret, that is the vision of hell and then what Our Lady said to them after that, were revealed much earlier.

It might seem harsh that Our Lady could show hell to such young children, but we have to remember that during the previous apparitions she had enveloped them in a mysterious "light from her hands," which somehow allowed them to experience God's love in a very direct way. And this vision of hell only lasted an instant, whereas they had also been told that they would be going to heaven. The vision of hell was really meant more as a reminder to humanity as a whole that hell does exist.

There was no apparition on 13th August because the children were kidnapped by the Mayor and for a short time thrown into gaol. They were threatened with being thrown into a cauldron of boiling oil if they did not reveal the secrets that the Lady had entrusted to them, but even this threat could not shake their resolve.

On Sunday 19th August, the Lady did appear to the children at a place called Valinhos, near Aljustrel. The Lady again asked the children to "pray, pray very much and make sacrifices for sinners; for many souls go to hell because there are none to sacrifice themselves and pray for them."

As I remember it, this was a very rocky terrain, one of the places we visited with the young English boy. He took us to some very demanding places, but being young and strong this posed no difficulty to me; for some of our party, though, including Mr de Kerckhove, it must have been very hard. I think that only a few of us visited these out of the way places, not least because some of our group were suffering from diarrhoea.

On Thursday 13th September, a crowd, estimated at about thirty thousand gathered in the Cova and the message from the Lady was much the same. This time however, she told the children that on 13th October Our Lord would come as well as Our Lady of Dolours and Our Lady of Mount Carmel, and that St. Joseph would appear with the Holy Infant to bless the world.

When the great day arrived, it is estimated that seventy thousand turned up to witness the promised miracle. The rain was torrential and the Cova was a sea of mud. A flash of light preceded the Lady's appearance and the children saw her in her usual place. Once again, Lucia asked, "What do you want of me?"

The Blessed Virgin responded: "I want to tell you that a chapel is to be built here in my honour. I am the Lady of the Rosary. Continue always to pray the Rosary every day. The War is going to end and the soldiers will soon return to their homes." She also said: "Do not offend the Lord our God anymore because He is already so much offended."

Our Lady then began to ascend towards the east, opening her hands as she had done during the first three apparitions. After she had disappeared, Lucia recounts that, "We beheld St. Joseph with the Child Jesus and Our Lady, robed in white with a blue mantle beside the sun. St. Joseph and the Child Jesus appeared to bless the world for they traced the Sign of the Cross with their hands. When, a little later the apparition disappeared, I saw I saw Our Lord and Our Lady. It seemed to me that it was Our Lady of Dolours. Our Lord appeared to bless the world as St. Joseph had done. This apparition also vanished and I saw Our Lady once more, this time resembling Our Lady of Mount Carmel."

There are many different accounts of what the spectators saw that day. Each person had their own memories of the miracle of the sun. The father of Francisco and Jacinta said this: "We looked easily at the sun, which did not blind us. It seemed to flicker on and off, first in one way and then the other. It shot rays in different directions and painted everything in different colours; the trees, the people, the air and the ground. What was most extraordinary was that the sun did not hurt our eyes at all. Everything was still and quiet and everyone was looking upwards. At a certain moment the sun seemed to stop and then began to move and dance until it seemed that it was being detached from the sky and was falling on us. It was a terrible moment."

After this tremendous miracle, Portugal—which was under an anti-Catholic regime—gradually recovered, as the ordinary Portuguese took the message of Fatima to their hearts.

12

My Lourdes Pilgrimage

Two people, who featured very largely in my memories of life in Forest Gate before the war, were Mary and James O'Reilly. They lived a stone's throw from St. Anthony's Church and we passed their house every day on the way to school. James and Mary had both tried their vocations to the religious life but, because of health problems, were unable to continue. So, Mary returned to her family home in Upton Park Road and at some stage, James became a lodger. Well, eventually, Mary's parents died and I suppose any brothers or sisters married and James and Mary were left alone. They had a special dispensation to marry, but to continue to live a chaste life.

Very often as we passed their house on the way to school, Mary would be standing at the gate and she plied us with holy pictures and little holy books. Even now I sometimes come across pictures with her name written on them in her big round handwriting "from Mary Josephine O'Reilly. Pray for me."

Mary was an artist and she had a studio upstairs at the back of the house overlooking the garden. The house was like something out of a Dickens' novel. The walls were covered with pictures so close together that you could barely put a pin between them. Their only means of heating and cooking were two oil-stoves. Every year we were invited in to see their crib. The remarkable thing about the crib was that the snow was made from hundreds of pins.

So what does all this have to do with Lourdes? Shortly before the outbreak of war, Mary took us up to her studio to see some paintings she had done of the shrine at Lourdes and the surroundings. I doubt if I would have known about the apparitions to St. Bernadette before seeing these paintings, and of course, during the war, pilgrimages from this side of the English Channel were not possible. It took some time after the end of war to organise pilgrimages again, and the first person that I recall making the pilgrimage to Lourdes as an invalid was one of our parishioners, Frank Twort.

In 1952, Frank went to Lourdes with the National Pilgrimage and, as one would expect, was overwhelmed by the whole experience. He was determined to make the pilgrimage again the following year and, when I discovered that it was just after my 21st birthday, I booked a place for myself. Sadly, Frank died before that date arrived, leaving behind a wife and four children.

The pilgrimage was led by Cardinal Griffin. Two train-loads of people left Cannon Street Station on the early morning of 12th May. It was still light when we crossed the English Channel and boarded another train that took us all the way to Lourdes. We travelled all through the night (sleeping in our seats) and arrived in Lourdes the following evening. I stayed at Hotel de la Grotte, sharing a room with an elderly lady from Barking. Her name was Mrs McCormack. I spent most of the time with two ladies with whom I had shared a compartment on the journey.

The pilgrimage itself followed the usual pattern, starting with Mass and followed by breakfast at which we were given the itinerary for the day. Mass had to precede breakfast because in those days we had to be fasting from midnight if we wanted to receive Holy Communion.

As far as I remember we spent part of the morning visiting some of the places of interest: the converted prison where the Soubirous family lived, the Boly mill where Bernadette's father worked, the convent where she lived after the apparitions, and many other places. Then we made our way down to the grotto where there was a constant flow of prayers in various languages. After spending some time in prayer we returned to the hotel for lunch. During the afternoon we returned to the Domain (the enclosure that separated the commercial part of the town from the religious part), and took part in the Blessed Sacrament procession and the Blessing of the Sick.

After our evening meal we took part in the torch-light procession during which the Rosary was recited and the Lourdes Hymn was sung. For many people this was the highlight of the day. Any spare time that we had during the

Mary (centre) on pilgrimage in Lourdes

day could be spent visiting some of the numerous souvenir shops or the cafés for a cup of coffee. Just before the close of the pilgrimage, all the English pilgrims assembled with Cardinal Griffin for a photograph.

The next time I went to Lourdes was in 1960, and that was with a small group of pilgrims organised by St. Christopher's Tours. I cannot remember what prompted me to go that time, because later, in October, I went to Oberammergau. Once more we travelled by train, but that time we spent a night in Paris, before boarding the train for Lourdes.

I shared a compartment with an Irish farmer and his wife, Mr and Mrs Taylor; an officer in the Royal Air-force who had been one of the Dambusters, whose name was Colin Brooke, and two Scottish ladies who were district nurses. One of them lived on an Island in the Outer Hebrides named South Uist. It is one of those places where everyone is Catholic. I think the other one lived in Fort William. One more person that I remember was an Irish lady who had a sweet shop in County Wicklow.

As far as the pilgrimage went, it followed much the same pattern as the National Pilgrimage. One thing that I do remember was hearing a sermon preached by Monsignor Vernon Johnson. I first learned about him when I read his book *One Lord, One Faith*. Fr. Vernon Johnson, as he was previously known, was a very "high" Anglican Vicar. He was not looking to become a Catholic, being perfectly happy in the Anglican Church, and he was very highly thought of by his fellow Anglicans.

Well, he paid a visit to Lisieux, the place associated with St. Therese and where her mortal remains are kept. Exactly what happened now escapes my memory, but from then on he was drawn towards the Catholic Church and after a long struggle felt compelled to answer the call and become a Catholic.

As was to be expected, the many Anglicans who held him in such high regard were devastated. That was why he wrote the book *One Lord, One Faith* as an apologia for the friends he was leaving behind. It was this book that was instrumental in bringing Leonard Cheshire into the Catholic Church. He was caring for a dying man, who must have been reading the book, and for want of anything better to do; Leonard Cheshire started reading it and was so impressed that he ended up becoming a Catholic.

On one of my holidays in Ireland I visited the Irish farmer and his wife, and the lady who ran the sweet shop came down to see me in Inglewood Road. She had kept in touch with Colin Brooke, who had resigned from the Air Force and tried his vocation for the priesthood. He was sent to the Beda College in Rome, but found it all too difficult, so he had not become a priest.

That would probably have been the last time I went to Lourdes if it hadn't been for a lady who always sat behind me at Mass on a Sunday, and who virtually pestered me to organise a pilgrimage from our parish. The difficulty was that she wouldn't fly or travel overnight. As it happened, very few people in our parish were interested and the neighbouring parishes all had their own pilgrimages, most of them flying. I had to tell the lady, whose name was Marcella that she would have to find an organised pilgrimage that fitted in with her requirements and book up with them. I ended up doing it for her and found a group in Coventry, who made the pilgrimage by coach every year and stopped overnight on the journey. They had five vacant places and I booked all of them, for Marcella and her friend Margaret, our daughter Catherine, and David and myself.

The coach coming down from Coventry had to make a detour to reach us at Crayford. Not surprisingly it arrived late, and Marcella turned up suffering from sciatica, while Catherine had a bad chest cold.

Being last on the coach we had no choice regarding our seats and I think it was Catherine who was very close to the toilet. The coach driver was obviously not familiar with the route in France and when it got dark he was still trying to find the place where we were to spend the night. When he did eventually find it, there was no food provided and it seemed to be in the middle of nowhere. Somewhere in the distance there was a McDonald's sign but too far away for us to reach. I cannot remember what we did that night, but we certainly did not have a dinner.

We eventually arrived in Lourdes and I think the hotel was quite comfortable. A wheel-chair was provided for Marcella and we did all the things that I had done on the previous two visits to Lourdes. We attended Mass in the enormous Basilica of St. Pius X that had not been there on my previous visits.

One afternoon we were taken by coach to a village not far from Lourdes called Betharram. Apparently this used to be a place of pilgrimage before Lourdes became so popular. Here in the Parish church is the (incorrupt) body of St. Michael Garicoits, who founded a religious organisation, the Society of Priests of the Sacred Heart of Betharram. The priest who was with our pilgrimage administered the Sacrament of the Sick to anyone in our party who wanted it, although the poor man was terminally ill himself.

On the homeward journey we spent a night in the Convent at Nevers, where St. Bernadette lived during her short life as a nun and where her incorrupt body is kept in the chapel. We were relieved when the coach arrived back in Crayford but pitied the rest of the pilgrims who still had to make the long journey back to Coventry. Marcella was very grateful that I had organised the pilgrimage for her and told me this repeatedly when we met her at Mass on Sundays.

13

Sybil Mary Magdalene Hart-Davis

Crayford is a town rich in history. According to the historians there was a settlement on Crayford Hill as far back as the stone-age. Across the road from St. Mary's Catholic church is the pre-reformation church of St. Paulinus. Mass was offered there as far back as the fifteenth century and the church was probably visited by St. John Fisher when he was Bishop of Rochester. With the Reformation, things changed. Christians continued to worship in the church, but the saying of the Mass was forbidden. It is probable, however, that the Catholic faith was kept alive by priests coming across from France and saying Mass in secret in some of the big houses in the district.

By 1840, Mass was again being offered on the site of St. Mary's and a new church was opened on 11th May 1842. It was that church, commonly referred to as the "old church" that held precious memories for so many of the present parishioners of St. Mary of the Crays: weddings, baptisms, First Holy Communions, Confirmations, Requiems… the list goes on.

During the two world wars, the faithful gathered round their priest to pray for peace, and the Rosary was recited every afternoon during the 1939-45 War. The church was damaged when St. Paulinus school, which stood on the site of St. Paulinus Court, was bombed. Later in the War, as I have related, the parish was shocked and saddened when seven members of the Ilott family were killed by one of the first

flying bombs to fall on Crayford. It was the Feast of the
Sacred Heart 1944. All these memories did not disappear
when the old church was demolished and neither should they.
History is about people—the people that we remember when
we say during the Mass: "Remember those who have died..."
It is in part to keep alive the memory of one of these
parishioners that I am writing this story.

Why should one person be singled out from many? Initially
because when Sybil Mary Magdalene Hart-Davis died, her
family presented the church with a memorial in the form of
carved wooden altar rails, to ensure that we would pray for
her. This was all the more significant because Sybil was a
convert to Catholicism and her only daughter, Deirdre,
followed her into the Church. It could not have been foreseen
at the time that altar rails would go out of fashion or even
that the old church would be demolished. When I realised
that there would be no place for the memorial in the church
as it is now, I felt obliged to do something to perpetuate the
memory of Sybil Hart-Davis.

Fr. McGettrick, the then parish priest, was not altogether
unsympathetic, but pointed out to me that no-one would
know who she was anyway. That was what prompted me to
find out something about her. My search culminated in a
letter from John Julius Norwich, who told me that Rupert
Hart-Davis had written a book about his mother. So, there
was indeed a story behind the altar rails.

The Hart-Davis family lived in Halcot House that stood in
a hundred acres of ground along Bourne Road, opposite Hall
Place in Bexley. Sybil Mary was the daughter of Lady Agnes
Cooper, the sister of Duff Cooper (the politician), sister-in-
law of Lady Diana Cooper (the actress), mother of Rupert
Hart-Davis, (the writer, publisher and editor), and of Deirdre,
and wife of Richard Hart-Davis. John Julius Norwich is her
nephew born two years after her death in 1927.

Born into an affluent family in 1885, Sybil Mary was a
twin. Her brother was still-born. She was very much the

victim of the society into which she was born, as most of us are. Married at seventeen to a man with whom she had little in common she had to learn the lesson that many learn who marry at an early age. The person one would marry at seventeen is not always the person one would choose at twenty-seven.

Those closest to her were killed in the First World War. In 1907 she gave birth to a son and two years later her daughter was born. No mother could have been more devoted to her children. Knowing that Rupert went to school at Eton, I did wonder before reading the book if he was really all that close to his mother. Children brought up by a nanny, and sent to boarding school at an early age, tend to be self-sufficient, or so I thought. The fact is that Rupert was away at school for nine years and during that time he wrote to his mother every day, and she to him.

I won't say too much about Sybil Mary's life here, but will concentrate on the last few years after she became a Catholic. Exactly what led her into the Catholic Church is not clear, but she was received into the Church by a Passionist, Fr. Vincent Logan, in Paris. He took the unusual step of receiving her without first giving a course of instruction. She wrote to Rupert on 2nd April 1923, "Last Friday I was re-christened and received into the Roman Catholic Church. It is the source of the greatest help, comfort and joy to me."

It was her dearest wish that Rupert would follow her into the Church, but as he so rightly said, it would have to have been from an inner conviction, which he did not possess. Sybil Mary added the name Magdalene to her name when she became a Catholic.

On returning to London, she went to the Dominican priory at Haverstock Hill for instruction. It was there that she fell under the influence of Fr. Bede Jarrett, who greatly impressed Rupert.

During the few short years that were left to her after her reception into the Church, Sybil entered into the Catholic life at Crayford. She became a handmaid of the Blessed Sacrament (one of those devotional organisations that one rarely hears of these days) and took her turn in cleaning the brasses.

In October 1923 she was confirmed at St. George's Cathedral Southwark. The following year, in late September, Deidre was received into the Church by a Fr. Carroll, "a darling old Irish Priest" with decided views on literature. Apparently he was a great admirer of G.K. Chesterton. In his book on his mother, Rupert writes, "He and my mother were devoted to each other and she, together with his housekeeper nursed him tenderly through his last illness in 1926." Sybil could not have known that her own death was but a year away.

The exact nature of her final illness is not very clear. It is evident that at times she was tormented with feelings of guilt over her past life, but that was probably a symptom of the illness itself. She also had terrible dreams and at times was unable to recognise those dearest to her.

At last, on 3rd January 1927, her long struggle was over. After her death Fr. Bede Jarrett wrote, "she was one of those, who was not so much interested in life, human and divine, as consumed by it, to whom religion is not so much a light as a flame. She was burnt up by that fire within."

If it was Fr. McGettrick's remark that prompted me to find out something about Sybil Mary, it was the sermon preached by Fr. Bede Jarrett on the occasion of the blessing of the altar rails that prompted me to pursue my search beyond what most people would deem necessary. Among other things he said: "Of this we are sure. She who loved beauty found it not as a secret, but as a Gospel; not as a thing hidden but as a friend revealed. It is therefore wholly fitting that those who loved her and whom she loved most have set up in her memory these Communion Rails."

14

Holidays in Scotland & Ireland

From the time I left school in 1948 until I married David in 1966, I had a holiday every year either on the Continent or in Ireland or Scotland. While I was working for the Australian Bank I very often had two holidays, as we were given an extra week for taking our holiday out of season. Having seen three Popes, Pius XII, John XXIII and Paul VI, I did not expect to see Pope John Paul II. However I did see him twice, with David. The first time was when he asked for families to pray with him. We went all the way by coach, and that journey was an adventure in itself. The second time we flew to Rome, when we attended a conference. By that time the Holy Father was very frail, but he celebrated Mass in St. Peter's Square, which we attended.

One of the most memorable holidays I had in Scotland was when I went to Iona. I had it in mind that I would like to see some of the Western Isles, not realizing that the best way to do this was to book a place on a cruise that would take in several of the islands.

I went by train from London to Oban, where I had booked a room in a hotel, and the following day I boarded the mail-boat that plied its way up the Sound of Mull to Tobermoray. Here it was moored for the night and made the return journey the following day. I spent the night in a hotel and early the next morning I boarded the boat again and went as far as

Craignure, where, according to a timetable I had acquired, a bus ran every day to the Iona ferry.

An open boat with an outboard motor ferried passengers to and from the mail-boat. Only a few people disembarked at Craignure. Among them was a young man who was on a rock-climbing expedition. I remembered him particularly because he resembled one of the parishioners at St. Mary's.

There was very little at Craignure, just the ferry-man's house, a small shop and a pub. I went into the shop and I think I purchased a few cards. The ferry-man must have been watching me and he came across and asked if he could help. When I told I was waiting for the bus for the Iona ferry, he said I would have a long wait, as it only ran in the evening. However, if I could wait until he put the wheel back on his car he was prepared to take me. I went into his house where his wife had just cooked some fresh scones and over a cup of tea and a lovely warm scone we chatted, mainly about the guests she had in the summer. With the car ready, we set off for the ferry. I was given a running commentary on the places we passed through, and on the inhabitants of the very few houses we passed on the way. Some of them were people who had spent their holidays in Mull for many years and then retired there. I met one such person on the return journey. The Iona Ferry also turned out to be an open boat with an outboard motor that was moored close to a place called Fionnphort.

When the ferry-man from Craignure dropped me off, he said he would book me a room in a hotel just a few miles along the road. I had to wait some time for the ferry to take me to Iona, but it was a glorious day and it was no hardship to sit on the rocks and admire the view. Again, only a few people made the crossing and I was left alone to find my way around.

There was just a small shop and a row of cottages and some distance away was the Abbey. Unfortunately, it was closed because the summer season was over, David and I did return many years later and had a good look round, but on that occasion I at least achieved my ambition to visit Iona, brief though my stay was.

A few people made the crossing back to Mull including the young man who had been rock-climbing. His holiday had been cut short when he sprained his ankle. Fortunately for him a doctor had been visiting the island that day and I think she organised a helicopter to take him back to the mainland.

I started to walk in the direction of Craignure, when I was overtaken by an elderly gentleman who had been on the ferry. He was a retired doctor who didn't think my leather brogue shoes were suitable for walking in the highlands. "Alright for Oxford Street", he said and offered me a lift in his car to my hotel. The small hotel was being run by an English girl who had only arrived the previous day. She cooked me a wonderful dinner, and I had a hot water bottle in my bed.

The following morning all hell was let loose in the form of a violent storm accompanied by gale-force winds. A travelling theatre had been visiting Mull and the small boat taking us out to the mail-boat was full to overflowing. It was all the ferry-man could do to keep the ferry in the right direction and some of the ladies in the theatre group were close to having hysterics. Eventually we arrived safely in Oban, and the comfort of the hotel that was my home for the duration of my holiday.

It might be worth mentioning that Tobermoray Bay is supposed to be where a galleon containing many treasures went down. I do not know if this story has ever been substantiated, but the name of Tobermoray bay had been familiar to me long before I went there.

Another event that I remember from that holiday was the cattle auction. All the cattle from the islands were brought in to Oban and driven through the main street to the auction room. This was because, with the impending bad winter, it would be difficult to feed them, especially if food was short. I was advised to look in on one of the auctions and I soon found out why. What with the Scottish accent of the auctioneer and the speed at which he spoke, I couldn't understand a word he said.

At the far end of Oban facing the sea, there is the Roman Catholic Cathedral. It is the seat of the Bishop of the diocese of Argyle and the islands.

The story of the Loch Ness Monster had always fascinated me so it was not surprising, that I should arrange a holiday in Inverness that is at one end of the loch. When I told one of my colleagues at the bank that I was going to Inverness and optimistically taking my jodhpurs with me, he told me of a pony-trekking hotel at Aviemore. Apparently the hotel was owned by a friend of one of the bank managers. As luck would have it they had a

Mary pony trekking in Scotland

vacancy for my first week. Accordingly I changed my plans and spent a week pony-trekking in the Cairngorms. The hotel provided us with a hearty breakfast and a packed lunch. We were shown how to saddle up our pony on the first day and how to use the reins and how to change from a walk to a trot. We followed a young lady who was in charge of us, climbing up some very rocky terrain and crossing streams and going into dense woodland. We took a break at mid-day for our lunch and each pony had a bag of hay while we enjoyed the delicious packed lunches provided by the hotel.

Among the members of our party was a young couple from Eltham. I sat with them at mealtimes and learned that the husband played golf at our local golf-course in Barnehurst just a stone's throw from our house in Inglewood Road.

The second week I spent in Inverness as planned. One day I went for a very long walk along the banks of the Ness, but the monster did not oblige me by appearing.

Many years later I spent a week in Fort William with my friend Christine and another friend, Mary Renn. We stayed in a bungalow overlooking Loch Linnhe. Every evening our landlady provided a delicious meal for us and the other guests. With the meal over, the drop leaf tables were folded up and put away and we spent the evening doing crosswords and exchanging stories. One of the guests was a prison warder.

Unfortunately it rained every day of our holiday, but we came away still vowing that we would return. I remember going to Fort Augustus and having to dry off in the Abbey.

Christine Hand and Mary Renn

Mary Renn was a Yorkshire girl but we became acquainted with her when she lived with her husband Leonard and their four children in Barnehurst. Leonard was Polish and had been subject to forced labour during the War. Under a government scheme he went to University over here after the War and became an economist. They moved away from Barnehurst to Eltham and Mary had two more children, Mary and Elizabeth. Although Mary was a wonderful mother, she yearned for something more than housework and cooking. I cannot remember whether she had been a teacher before she married but she eventually turned to teaching and taught in Eltham, Sidcup and Gravesend. Occasionally Christine and I would spend an evening with her at her house in Eltham. It was Mary who first introduced us to chow mein.

Sadly, while she was still teaching Mary fell a victim to cancer and died. Her death was a great blow to Christine who spent many happy holidays with her, right up to the time of her death.

My holidays in Ireland are too numerous to recount in detail, so I will just touch on a few events that I think worth mentioning.

When I was nineteen I spent two weeks in Dun Laoghaire with my brother Rory. We stayed in a guest house and went out every day, mainly on bus tours arranged by C.I.E. Most of the tours were of places south of Dublin in the Wicklow Mountains, but on one occasion we went with another coach company that took us north to such places as Tara, Newgrange, Monasterboice, and Drogheda, the scene of the battle of the Boyne. Rory was a great mimic and he enjoyed taking off some of the Irish characters we met, such as the old man who let us in to the Newgrange Tumulus.

It was during this holiday that that we had a conversation on the top of a bus going from Dublin to Dun Laoghaire. We were looking back over our lives and Rory told me how happy he had been at Mark Cross, the Junior Seminary. So happy in fact, that his best friend Brian Glover had followed him. Brian was a year or two older than Rory and they had both been at Dartford Grammar School. This conversation should dispel any rumours that there may have been that Rory was at Mark Cross under duress and under pressure from our parents.

On two occasions I took my bike to Ireland and travelled all round the Midlands where it is relatively flat. I wanted to find the place my ancestors came from. I got as far as Roscommon when I made a phone call to Fr. O'Grady who was close by at Lanesborough. Sensing that I was a bit under the weather he invited me to spend the rest of my holiday with him, which I did. He took me to Knock, where in 1879 two local women and thirteen more onlookers saw an apparition of Our Blessed Lady, St. John and St. Joseph. Every year at least a million and a half pilgrims visit the shrine and Pilgrims have included Pope John Paul II and Mother Teresa.

Every year, at the end of July or the beginning of August, photos appeared in the Catholic Papers of a long procession of people climbing a mountain. That mountain is Croagh

Patrick, Ireland's holy mountain. The people were making a pilgrimage to the top of the mountain, which is 2,510 ft. high; it is believed that in AD 441 St. Patrick spent 40 days in prayer and fasting there, for the Irish people. From the photos, it looks as though there is a path up the mountain, but the reality is rather different. I had the rather mad idea that I would be able to climb Croagh Patrick alone, as I had never been in Ireland at the time of the national pilgrimage. It was fine at the beginning but the higher I went up the more difficult it became. When I was about half-way up I turned round and, horror of horrors, I realised that the downward journey was more frightening than the upward trek. Also If I had an accident, no-one would know where I was and I could have lain there for days. With the help of my guardian angel I managed to climb down without any trouble. I learned a lesson that day!

During my stay in Westport I visited the Island of Achill, Ireland's largest island. I saw only a very small part of it. There were donkeys roaming free on the beach and I took some photos of them. I went into a bar for a drink of lemonade and the man behind the counter told me that for many years he had worked in the Old Kent Road.

While I was waiting on Westport Railway Station on my way home, a young girl came running up to me and asked if I was going to England. Her name was Patsy O'Toole and she came from one of the islands off the West Coast. In fact, all the people on the island were O'Tooles. She was on her way to her sister's wedding that was to take place in Birmingham, and this was Patsy's first visit to the mainland. All the houses on the island where she lived were bungalows so she was not acquainted with stairs. Unfortunately I couldn't stay with her for the whole journey because I was travelling first class on the boat, but I feared for her safety. She said that her mother was crying when she left the island because she knew that in all probability, Patsy would not return.

There are many more stories that I could tell about Ireland; people I met, places I visited. However these memoirs would not be complete without a mention of my visit to Lough Derg. Situated in North-west Ireland it is close to the border between the North and Co. Donegal. I spent the night before I visited the island in Sligo. I had read that a bus ran between Sligo and the Lough, but with hindsight I would guess that this was not the easiest way to go.

So what is so special about Lough Derg? Well it is not the Lough itself, but an island that is situated close to the southern shore and is known as Station Island. As with Croagh Patrick, there is an association with St. Patrick who is said to have spent forty days on the island praying that Ireland would be rid of evil spirits. Thousands of people every year make a penitential pilgrimage to Station Island during the period from the 1st June and 15th August. As well as a Basilica and hostels for the pilgrims, there are a number of circles of stones around which the pilgrims walk, bare footed, while reciting specific prayers. I remember fasting from the night before, all the following day and all the first night that we spent in prayer. In the corner of the complex there was a small room where there was a large vat of hot water from which we were allowed to drink. This was to prevent pilgrims from being sick, and as a special concession pepper was sprinkled on the mugs of water. When I first saw the water, I thought it was soup because it was a browny yellow colour, but that evidently was the colour of the water on the island.

Some people find the fasting too difficult and they have to leave the island. I overheard priests who were discussing a girl who had been sick and was having to leave. One of the priests was pleading her cause, saying it was very difficult for some young people. I think the outcome was that if they relaxed the rules for one, it wouldn't stop there.

At some stage, I cannot remember just when, we were allowed a mug of black tea and a slice of dry toast, referred to as "black bread". Never did dry bread taste so delicious! After being up all the first night, I couldn't wait to get to bed on the second night. The little nun in charge of the dormitory where I slept told me that usually she was a nurse at St. Anthony's Hospital, Cheam. That was where our organist from St. Mary's had died and I asked her if she remembered him. She told me that she did.

The whole pilgrimage lasted three days and the fast had to be kept up for the rest of the day after we had left the island. As well as the hardship of the fast, walking barefoot on the stones and going without sleep, many people suffered from the intense cold. Some were wearing two or three coats. I was fortunate that I wore a suede jacket and a nylon Mac, and the Mac seemed to keep out the cold.

An open boat took us from the island to the mainland and, I think a bus took us to Omagh, the town that has become famous after so many people were killed by the bomb in 1998. I remember going into a café and asking for a slice of dry toast, much to the surprise of the man behind the counter. That is how I know that we still had to fast that day. Omagh, of course, is part of Northern Ireland and it is the only time I went north of the border. A train took me from Omagh to Dublin and my pilgrimage was over.

15

My Friend Pamela

My friend from those years, Pamela Sheldrake, died in 2001. She was in hospital, expecting to be discharged, but she died of a blood clot. She was just over a month younger than myself but she didn't live to see her 69th birthday. We had been friends for sixty years and never a day passes without my thinking of her. My friendship with Pamela had a terrific impact on my life and for that reason I feel impelled to write about our years together.

Pamela was the granddaughter of Mr and Mrs Hitchcock who lived next door to our school. Mr Hitchcock had been coachman to the Evans family who lived in Shenstone, a large house that stood where the school for handicapped children now stands in Old Road, Crayford. Mr and Mrs Hitchcock raised nine children in the little cottage-type house next to the school. Pamela's mother, Dorothy, was one of the oldest. The others were: Winifred, Bob, Bert, Charlie, Percy, Ronnie, Kathleen and Margaret.

When I first knew Pamela, the coach-houses, stalls, harness room and other buildings were still in good repair. Either side of the yard between the cottage and the big house, chickens roamed the yard at will and cows grazed in the parkland. Beyond the yard and behind the Catholic church was a walled garden, at that time tended by Pamela's grandfather.

Both the Evans and the Hitchcock families attended St. Paulinus C. of E. Church and the Hitchcock children, and Pamela and her brother Grant, attended St. Paulinus School. At the beginning of the Blitz in 1940, St. Paulinus School was bombed, and Pamela and Grant joined us at St. Joseph's (RC) School. Soon after, Pamela's father died, making it necessary for her mother to take a permanent job. This meant, of course, that Pamela and Grant spent most of the school holidays with their grandparents. The whole of Shenstone Park was their playground, but Mrs Hitchcock decided, in her wisdom, that Pamela should have some friends from school to keep her company. That was how our friendship began.

Christine and I were invited to spend the afternoons playing in the park with Pamela and Grant, taking with us a picnic tea. I think Christine only came with us for the first summer, but Pamela and I took advantage of every school holiday to live in a world of make-believe in Shenstone. One of Pamela's uncles trained horses and was acquainted with the family of Alan Oliver, the British show jumping rider and course designer. Pamela and Grant had stayed with him and his wife during the Blitz, so many of our pretend games centred on horse riding and gymkhanas.

When it was very hot, we took off our shoes and socks and dangled our legs in any of the three tanks of water provided for the cows. We often thought what a pity it was that Shenstone did not have a stream running through it. At a certain time each year the grass would be cut and built into a haystack.

When we were ten years old, Christine Hand and I sat for the scholarship. We were the only two girls to enter for it that year and the result of passing was a place at St. Joseph's Convent Grammar School at Abbeywood. Pamela was not allowed to enter for it by the school, but her mother insisted and she sat privately at Dartford County Girls School. As it happened, Pamela did not pass, but the Freemasons paid for her to go on to St. Joseph's Convent. Christine and I were placed in the same class, but Pamela was in another class. She seemed to settle down very well, making her own friends, but meeting me at lunchtimes. I must admit that initially I was very unhappy at St. Joseph's. It seemed so big after our little primary school in Crayford. We had to stay for dinner and in the winter it was always very cold.

For a time we continued to play in Shenstone during the holidays and some of Pamela's school friends joined us. I remember one girl, Elsie Eels (whose parents ran a fish shop in Belvedere) came along, and later we went to tea at her house.

During our second year at St. Joseph's, the allied forces invaded France, and soon after, Germany launched the "flying bombs" on South-east England. This immediately put a stop to our school attendance and once again, Pamela and Grant were sent away to the country. The flying bombs did not last very long because the allied forces were gradually taking over the launching sites.

When I learned that Pamela had returned, I went round to her grandmother and we decided to go out in the park to play. In the short time that Pamela had been away, something had happened to both of us. We could no longer make-believe. I suppose it was the first step towards growing up.

Other things, more drastic were soon to take place. Mr Hitchcock died and Shenstone was bought by the Council, including the surrounding land that was made into a public park. The cottage and yard with the coach houses were bought by the Catholic church for the extension of St. Joseph's school. Pamela's grandmother and her daughter Margaret were given a three-bedroomed house in Oakwood Drive, just around the corner from where I lived in Inglewood Road. Pamela's mother decided to leave their cottage in Watling Street and live with her mother and sister. There was also an uncle, who was not married and for whom the house in Oakwood Drive was home. About this time, Mrs Hitchcock's youngest son, Ronnie, died of T.B. It must have been heart-breaking for her, losing her husband, her son and also her home. However, the family settled down to life in their new home and it was actually easier living in a modern house. The old cottage had no water supply in the house: the water tap was across a small yard, between the house and the harness room.

Having Pamela living round the corner was great for me and I'm sure it was good for her too. Our games of make-believe at last turned into reality for Pamela, when she started having riding lessons from a Mr Clace. The lessons took place in a field at the side of Russell Stoneham Maternity Home. It was all part of the Russell Stoneham Estate. I cannot

remember now just when Pamela and Grant started having the riding lessons, but I think it must have been while Pamela was still at school. She was always anxious that I would also enjoy her passion for horses and eventually I acquired a pair of land-army breeches and

Pamela with her horse

arranged for Mr Clace to take me on. This must have been after I had left school because there was no question of my parents paying for riding lessons, and I remember going to Harry Hall's after work to buy my hard hat. It was through these sessions with Mr Clace that Pamela met Janet Gale who lived in Hillingdon Road, close to Oakwood Drive. Janet was a pupil at Stonyhurst Convent, a private school in Watling Street, where St. Catherine's School now stands.

During the War there were no local gymkhanas, but as things gradually got back to normal these events were again held in Bexley and Bromley. Pamela and I took it all very seriously, armed with our programmes and pencils. Pamela, of course, was the expert, but I did my best to make sensible comments. I must say that Pamela was always very tolerant of my ignorance of such things as horses, wild-life, birds, flowers etc. I began asking my parents for books on birds and country life in an effort to gain some knowledge of the things that Pamela seemed to know all about. My proudest possession was a book entitled, *The Countryside Companion*. It was about life on the farm and also had photos of wild flowers, trees, shrubs etc., to enable the reader to identify the various species. To this day I still use that book, mainly in solving clues in my weekly general knowledge crossword.

When I was eleven years old and starting at St. Joseph's Convent, my brother Rory went away to St. Joseph's College, Mark Cross, near Tunbridge Wells. I had been asking my parents if I could have a dog for some time, but they had always refused my request. I was quite surprised when my mother bought Micky, a mongrel pup of six weeks. He was to be a consolation for Rory leaving home.

Pamela would have liked a dog but it was out of the question while they were living in the cottage in Watling Street. When the family moved to Oakwood Drive, her mother bought her a spaniel. I cannot remember the name of the dog, but later on, Pamela had a black Labrador named Trudie, and it is that dog that I remember most. Trudie was a very boisterous dog, difficult to handle, so Pamela took her to dog-handling classes. I expect that Micky would have benefited from attending such classes, but by then he was old and did not have much longer to live.

When Pamela's class hired a coach and went to Crufts Dog Show, I went with them. Pamela was always anxious for me to join in all her activities, and as I loved dogs anyway I was only too pleased to go to Crufts. I had never seen so many dogs of all shapes and sizes. We watched the obedience trials for some time. My favourite was a border collie: perhaps he reminded me of the last dog my grandmother had. She became unable to give him sufficient exercise so he went to live with a man in the country.

The second time I went to Crufts was not so enjoyable. By then I think Micky had died and we were thinking of the possibility of a replacement. I decided that I would like a golden retriever, so we took down some names of breeders. However, when my father knew of my intentions, he absolutely forbade me to purchase another dog and even said if Pamela turned up with one he would insist on her taking it away. This was partly because we were all broken-hearted when Micky died. He always went to the post box with my mother when she wrote her weekly letter to Rory, and after Micky died she would go up to the post box with tears streaming down her face hoping she would not meet any of our neighbours.

In addition, my father did not want to be landed with the job of taking another dog for walks, as I am afraid he had had to do with Micky. Not that I never took him out, but for various reasons it often fell to my father. In 1947 we went for a holiday in Ireland and put Micky into kennels, but he fretted so much that my mother vowed she would never leave him again. So, for years they never had a holiday, and that was another reason for not wanting another dog.

Naomi and Alf Coshall were two people who had a common bond in their love of horses and riding. Alf owned a large horse called "Sprite" and a smaller horse, with a long, flowing mane called "Copper", while Naomi owned "Georgie". All three horses grazed in the Russell Stoneham grounds, but in the bad weather Copper and Sprite were stabled in the Vicarage stables. Georgie had a stable in Naomi's garden up on Dartford Heath. Naomi had been a member of the Civil Service Riding Club. Well, Naomi and Alf decided to get married and, somehow, Pamela and Janet Gale were roped in to look after the horses while they were on their honeymoon.

That was the beginning of a long friendship and as usual I became involved. When I first started riding lessons Mr Clace was teaching me as well as Pamela and Grant. He was quite an elderly man, although he had a young wife and a little daughter named Elizabeth. I think it must have been due to ill-health that Mr Clace gave up the riding lessons, or he may have died. Anyway, I continued riding on Copper and Georgie. It was Naomi who gave me instructions and one day decided that it would be good for me to ride without stirrups. Well, I fell off and for a few minutes could not remember anything. Because I was her responsibility, Naomi took me to Erith Hospital where they kept me in for a week. I think this was partly because they had previously discharged Alf after a fall, and he had in fact, broken his wrist.

Every Sunday afternoon, Pamela and I went for a long walk across Dartford Heath. At the top of Station Road there was a large detached house where the Lyle family lived. The Lyles owned the local lemonade factory. The house was surrounded by a stone wall, and as we passed by, the nose of a Boxer dog would appear over the wall. It turned out that his name was Samson. His owner was Josie, one of the Lyle daughters and somehow she joined the little group of riders down at Russell Stoneham. I suppose Naomi and Josie were at least acquaintances if not actual friends by reason of the fact that they were neighbours, although the Lyle house was surrounded by a large garden with a tennis court.

Eventually, Pamela bought a pony of her own. I suppose that was inevitable. He was called "Candle" and was unbroken. Pamela took on the difficult task of breaking him in, and at times was "black and blue" with the bruises she sustained from being thrown off. Eventually she did succeed in breaking him in, but no-one else could ride him. On one occasion, Agnes McCall, an old school friend, came down for the day and Pamela, unwisely I thought, suggested that she have a ride on Candle. Poor Agnes was very excited, but no sooner was she seated on the pony than he took off and tipped her into a sand pit. As a result Agnes had to take a week off work.

Josie also bought a pony, only to find him/her dead one Sunday morning. There were some yew-trees in the area and the pony must have eaten some of the cuttings. Yew is a deadly poison to animals. Keeping a horse, even if it is in a field, is a very demanding hobby: they have to be fed and groomed and particularly cared for in the cold weather. Because the horses sometimes went out into the road, they had to be regularly shod, and if they showed signs of being unwell, the vet had to be called.

Close to the paddock were some brick buildings that had housed the soldiers who operated the gun emplacement during WW II. Pamela tried to coax Candle into one of the buildings during a particularly severe winter, but Candle wasn't having any of that. Consequently, Pamela had to do her best to make some kind of shelter out of branches. He didn't seem to be any the worse for having to winter out of doors.

Naomi was an avid follower of the national and international horse shows. On several occasions during the big shows, she rented a hotel room for the week, within easy reach of the venue. Each day she would invite a different friend to attend the horse show and then share the hotel room for the night. On at least two occasions I was Naomi's guest. She had tickets for the members' enclosure and I remember the Queen presenting one of the trophies. I think it must have been the King George V trophy that was at stake.

My parents never had a television, so I suppose show jumping was a novelty to me. It is certainly something I would never have seen in the flesh if it had not been for my friendship with Pamela.

While Pamela and Grant were at school, they always went away with their mother, Dorothy, for a summer holiday. Usually it was to a sea-side resort, sometimes to the Isle of Wight. When Grant left school and went to work on a farm, Pamela continued to go on holiday with her mother. This was one aspect of our lives that we did not share. As I have related, in 1950, I went to Rome with a party from our church organised by Fr. Patrick Cox. This gave me a taste for foreign travel and for many years thereafter, I went on an organised tour or sometimes a pilgrimage to the various shrines of

Europe. I also managed to visit Ireland on many occasions, and also Scotland.

My friend Pamela would have enjoyed coming with me on some of my Irish and Scottish holidays, but she would not disappoint her mother. One year they hired a horse-drawn caravan in Ireland with Josie and travelled around the leafy lanes of Co. Cork. Only on one occasion did we holiday together and that also was in Ireland. It was a walking holiday, starting in Dublin and ending in Galway. Not that we walked all the way. We spent some time in Cong, the place where the film, "The Quiet Man," was shot. We then walked to Clifden, the capital of Connemara. I remember being quite short with Pamela, because my feet were blistered and she still insisted on walking to the sea: she had to do that walk alone while I recovered. One year, Pamela and Dorothy went to Switzerland. For some reason I do not think it was a great success. Pamela said it was alright, but she would not want to go there again.

Grant lived away from home working as a herdsman, but when he was eighteen he was called up into the Air Force to do his national service. Margaret, the youngest member of the Hitchcock family married Alec Nunn and not very long after that, Mrs Hitchcock died. It is impossible for me to quote dates for these events, but I know that by the time Margaret married, Grant was showing signs of his illness and Percy, Pamela's uncle, was in the early stages of M.S. Eventually he went to live in the Star and Garter home for ex-service men. His illness became progressively worse, but he lived for many years.

Pamela and I saw each other most weekends. After I fell off the horse I lost my enthusiasm for riding, but I still went up to the paddock on Sunday morning and then we would go for our long walk on Sunday afternoon.

One year we signed up for the handicraft class at Manor House, Crayford, Kent. I cannot remember just who was in our little group, but I think it comprised Pamela and Josie and

I believe Janet Gale, and myself. Pamela made a tapestry fire-screen, I did some Assisi embroidery and someone else made soft toys. It was a good opportunity for a chin-wag as well as doing something constructive. By this time things at home were very depressive for Pamela and she was glad to get out in the evening.

Although Pamela seemed quite content with her life we did hope, for many years that we would both meet the right young man and settle down. When the Vet made scathing remarks about "women and their horses"

Five friends from the fifties

Pamela and Josie always insisted that they were a substitute for the children they did not have. I remember walking through Bexley Village and discussing with Pamela how many children we would like to have. Four seemed to be a good number and as it happened that was the number I had. Pamela had one less.

When we went for our regular Sunday afternoon walks, we invariably passed a young man named David on his way to play the organ at St. Mary's Church. I always called across to him, little knowing that one day he would be my husband, the father of those four children I had hoped to have.

I never knew just when Pamela started to see John Winkworth on a regular basis. Because she was so involved with Candle, I thought that when I saw less of her at weekends it was because she was going to local events with Josie and Naomi. It was a pity that she did not feel she could confide in me about her friendship, although I can understand why she did not. By the time I married, Pamela and John already had William, and were unable to attend my wedding because Jennifer's birth was imminent.

Like her mother, Pamela suffered the pain of widowhood after John died of leukaemia. She also had her own illness and also the illnesses of her other son, Timothy, to contend with.

The last time we met, she called in with a plant for my birthday. As we chatted across the table I remember her saying that in spite of all the difficulties, she felt that she had had a good life. Pamela invariably had a smile on her face. That is the way I shall always remember her.

Dorothy (Pamela's mother), had three sisters; Margaret, the youngest of the Hitchcock family, Kathleen, also one of the youngest members, and Winifred who was one of the oldest. Mrs Hitchcock used to tell me that Winnie was more or less brought up in the presbytery just a few yards along the road. She also recalled that during the First World War, they were all taking shelter under a large table in the presbytery when a shell came through the wall.

Unlike her older sister, Winnie, Kathleen was very close to her mother and sisters in Oakwood Drive. I saw her from time to time, and she married a farmer named Harold. They had one child, Anne, and lived on a farm in Ripley, Surrey. Pamela and I spent a weekend on that farm, which was reputed to be haunted. The farmhouse was hundreds of years old and had once been part of a monastery. The ruins of an abbey still stand in one of the fields. I remember being scared at night in case the ghost paid us a visit. The other thing that remains in my mind is the enormous number of pigs that Harold was raising.

Pamela's uncle Bert also lived in a house that was reputed to be haunted. Bert lived with his wife and son and daughter in the lodge of a big house near Farningham in Kent. He was the gardener and the house went with the job. Pamela and I paid him a visit once on our bikes, but that was the only occasion that I recall meeting him, except, of course at Margaret's wedding.

Charlie, one of the Hitchcock's sons kept a greengrocers shop in Bexley Village. Sometimes, we would take freshly picked mushrooms from Shenstone for him to sell.

Like Kathleen. Charlie and his wife had one child, a daughter, Sheila. The main thing that I remember about

Charlie was that he kept racing pigeons. He gave us a very instructive tour of his lofts one evening. Sadly, Charlie died suddenly, before his mother, another great sadness for Mrs Hitchcock.

I do not remember whether Pamela had any strong views on fox-hunting. On one occasion she did ride with the Westerham hunt and had her photo in the *Horse and Hound* along with Janet Gale. Which horses they rode and how they transported them I cannot remember. I doubt if Candle would have been sufficiently disciplined to ride with the hunt.

Pamela spent most of her married life in Broadstairs so we did not see each other very often during those years. It is a pity that we never knew each other's children and kept in touch mainly through the occasional letter.

I knew that after John's death, she kept herself busy by looking after donkeys and working in a nursery. She did not make much of her illness (colitis) and also the fact that Timothy was schizophrenic. However, Timothy did attend hospital and was under medication, unlike Grant who had a similar problem.

The Hitchcock family were people of great faith and Pamela never lost this in spite of the ups and downs of life. In one of her letters to me she related how she and an old lady were delivering the Gospel of St. John to all the people on a council estate as a celebration of the Millennium. She was surprised at the kind reception they received. Seeing Pamela's smiling face at the door probably had something to do with that. I think of my friend every day and as I am also a person of great faith, trust that one day we will meet again in heaven.

Although the Hitchcock's had such a large family, they had comparatively few grandchildren. Three of their sons, Ronald, Percy and Bob had no children. Bert had two children and Charlie had one daughter. Of the girls, Kathleen had one daughter, Dorothy had two and Margaret, the youngest, had three children. Winifred, who always lived in the North of England and seemed to have very little contact with the family did have children, but I do not know how many.

So, when Pamela died, there were few relatives around to attend her funeral, except of course, her own children. Margaret and Alec Nunn were the only ones to make the journey to Broadstairs. I was unable to go because there was a thick fog that day and it would have been unwise to venture onto the motorway. Margaret told me that she was surprised at the large number of friends Pamela had made, and this made up for the lack of relatives.

Timothy subsequently went into a residential home. Jennifer was expecting her second child although still not married, and William, her other son, was living with a partner in Ilfracombe. Unfortunately they would never have known the cottage where their great grandparents and grandmother spent much of their lives; or the parkland of Shenstone where their mother and Uncle Grant spent so many happy hours of their childhood. My children, on the other hand, played every day in a corner of Shenstone that formed part of the playground of St. Joseph's Primary School. They also passed the old cottage, and my grandson Michael tells me that he climbs trees in Shenstone while he is waiting to collect his little sister, 'Cesca, from school. Maybe he will be the last of a generation who have connections with Shenstone, but hopefully through these pages it will not be forgotten.

16

Aylesford Priory

It was a bright, sunny day in the year 1949, when a little group of people from the Parish of St. Mary of the Crays boarded a train in Dartford, bound for Aylesford. With their curate, Fr Paddy Cox, they were making what would prove to be one of the first pilgrimages to Aylesford Priory, recently acquired by the Carmelites after centuries in non-Catholic hands.

The history of the Friars, as the Priory is now known, goes back over 700 years, when the Carmelite friars were brought to England by Sir Richard Grey, a crusading nobleman and Sir John Vesey.

The Friars, from across the River Medway

The Carmelites were originally hermits and came from Palestine, but in 1247, St Simon Stock was elected Prior General and it is thought that he was responsible for changing the Order from an eremitical way of life (as hermits) to that of a mendicant (or begging) brotherhood.

The brotherhood was under the special patronage of Our Lady and according to a tradition, while Simon Stock was praying to our blessed Mother, she appeared to him in a vision with many angels and the scapular, which is part of the habit worn by the Friars, in her hand. She promised salvation for him and all Carmelites who wore it, saying: "This will be for you and for all Carmelites the privilege, that he who dies in this will not suffer eternal fire."

The Brown Scapular as we now have it is a sacramental worn around the neck, comprised of two pieces of brown cloth. The Scapular promise implies that the Blessed Virgin will intercede to ensure that the wearer of the Scapular obtains the grace of final perseverance, that is of dying in a state of grace, and this privilege has now been extended to all Catholics who are enrolled in the Scapular.

Statue of Our Lady and St Simon Stock at Aylesford

Eventually, in the year 1248, a new church was completed and on the 31st August was dedicated to Blessed Mary, Mother of God.

Over the years, more and more important people visited the Priory, making large donations that were spent on the development of the Cloister Building and the replacement of the original church by one of rag-stone. It became a stopping-off place for pilgrims on their way to Canterbury.

Sadly, in the year 1539, the friars were forced to leave because of the Reformation and did not return until 410 years later, in 1949, when the community was re-established under the then Prior, Fr. Malachy Lynch.

It wasn't long after that when we arrived on that sunny Sunday morning. The place was deserted except for a few volunteers who were sleeping on camp-beds in an upper room. We ate our sandwiches under a tree close to where the holy water stoup now stands. Where the church had once stood was a pile of stones, but the cloister chapel was intact, and contained the Blessed Sacrament.

Fr. Malachy was one of three Irish brothers, all Carmelites, all of whom now lie buried in the Priory grounds. However, in

Fr Malachy Lynch with pilgrims

1949 he had the tremendous task of rebuilding the Shrine. He was absolutely convinced that Our Lady had appeared to St. Simon Stock at Aylesford. I heard him say many times that the only dispute was whether the apparition occurred at Aylesford or at Cambridge. Because the Friars left Cambridge of their own accord he reasoned that they would never have done so if Our Lady had appeared there. However, at Aylesford they had to be forced to go.

After that first visit with Fr. Cox, our Parish priest, Fr. Brendan Byrne made any excuse to hire a coach and take as many parishioners as it would hold to go to Aylesford. We saw the shrine grow from a pile of stones to the wonderful building that we see today.

We were there for all the big events, including the return of the skull of St. Simon Stock from Bordeaux. I remember seeing the tall figure of Eamon de Valera (first Prime Minister of the Republic of Ireland) among the crowds that day.

Being quite a keen cyclist in my youth, I made many private visits on my bike—Aylesford is about 20 miles from Barnehurst. My parents would also have a day out and go down on the train. On one of my visits I was enrolled in the Brown Scapular by Fr. Malachy Lynch.

In an earlier chapter of this book I related how my parents were able to buy their house when the owner offered it to them at a ridiculously low price, because that was all they could afford.

After they had been told by his bank that the Rev. Dentith (the owner) wanted to sell the house, they paid a visit to

Aylesford. It wasn't really with that intention in mind, but while they were there they left a petition in the box provided in the chapel where the skull of St. Simon Stock is kept. I didn't know exactly what they said, but it was to do with the house. Sometime later, on the 16th July (Feast of our Lady of Mount Carmel), my mother was about to leave for morning Mass, when the postman delivered a letter with a Jersey postmark. This could only have been from one person and fearing that it was bad news, Mother was tempted to leave it until she returned from Mass. Bracing herself for the worst, she opened the letter, which was from the Rev. Dentith offering the house at a price they could afford.

David and I also had an unusual experience on another 16th July. Again, it was to do with a house.

When we married, we bought a house in Old Bexley Village, close to the shops and the Catholic Church. At that time a plot of land had been bought that was intended for the building of a Catholic Primary School which would be ready within four years. Within the first four years of our marriage, we had four children, but it seemed as though the school was not going to materialise.

My Wedding Day

We started to look for a suitable house within walking distance of our old school, St. Joseph's in Crayford. It was at a time when houses were sold even before they were advertised. We were trying to sell our old house in order to purchase a newer one and the task seemed impossible. Every house that we went for was sold within two weeks, so after several disappointments we gave up trying.

Then on the 16th July, (probably in 1971), David was on holiday from his job at the Wellcome Foundation and we were having a leisurely breakfast, when a man from Kirrage

Jones, the Estate Agent at the corner of our road, knocked at our door. He had found a house, advertised privately in the local paper, that suited our requirements, and the vendors were prepared to wait. There and then we drove round to 18 Eastleigh Road, and viewed the house that was to be our home for the next 36 years.

Pilgrims at Aylesford Shrine

Whenever David and I return to Crayford from our home in the East Midlands, we always make a point of visiting Aylesford and saying the fifteen decades of the Rosary as we walk round the Rosary Way. This year, it coincided with our 46th wedding anniversary. With our four children (now all in their forties) and our eight grand-children we have many intentions to pray for and many blessings for which to say "thank you".

Incidentally, without any planning on our part, we moved into our present home on the feast of Our Lady of Fatima.

17

Rory and my Parents

My brother Rory was born on 28th April 1930, and baptised Roderick Joseph. Our father really wanted to name him Rory after an Irish patriot, Rory O'Connor, who died during the troubles, when Ireland was fighting for independence. However, he discovered that Rory O'Connor's name was Roderick, and Roderick was the name of a saint, whereas Rory was not.

Like Rory O'Connor he was always known as Rory and right up the time of his death, in writing to me, he always signed himself "Rory".

From a very early age , Rory expressed a wish to be a priest, long before he had any close association with priests, and we only attended Mass once a week on Sunday. Our house in Forest Gate was 1¾ miles from the church, so it was not possible for mother to attend daily Mass as she did when we moved to Barnehurst. By that time Rory was nine years old and he was trained to be an altar server. As I have said elsewhere in this book, the curates, and particularly Fr. Duffy, were frequent visitors to our house, and it is not surprising that they were interested in this young boy who wanted to be a priest.

When the bishop, (Bishop Amigo), visited the parish, the altar servers were introduced to him and Rory was introduced as the boy who wanted to be a priest. I remember Rory saying that the bishop held his hand. Subsequently, when he was thirteen, Rory went to the Junior Seminary at Mark Cross. He was so forward in his Latin that he skipped the first class, and one of the professors said he was one of the cleverest boys he had ever taught.

Throughout all his years at the seminary (five years at Mark Cross, and six years at St. John's Seminary, Wonersh) Rory wrote home every week. His letters were always happy, witty, informative, and I can only say, remarkable. For many years my mother kept them and only destroyed them because of a lack of space. Mother always said that if there were any hint of him being unhappy, he would be home like a shot and no questions asked.

Well, in due course he was ordained at St. John's Seminary and offered his first Mass at our Parish Church of St. Mary's. It was a great joy for the parish. Many of the parishioners had known him since he was a young boy, and followed his progress through his studies at the seminary. After their ordination, most of the young priests went to parishes as curates, but because he was extra clever, Rory and three others were sent to Cambridge University to get a degree.

Rory read English Literature and having obtained his degree, was sent with the three others to teach at a boys' boarding school near Guildford. I cannot remember him ever complaining, but this was obviously not what he had intended when he became a priest. After ten years, he was given a parish in Surrey. He would have been quite happy to go as a curate somewhere, as he had no experience as a parish priest, but Bishop Cashman insisted that he have a parish. At the time our old parish priest said it would be a disaster, and so it proved to be.

Addlestone was a very difficult parish, with no church and a number of Mass Centres. It had previously been served by a Religious Order. It proved to be more than Rory could cope with alone and, after appealing a number of times to the bishop for help, he threw in the towel and left the priesthood. I doubt but he was one of the last priests to be laicised before

Pope John Paul II clamped down on it, meaning that any priest leaving the priesthood could not marry in the Church.

Rory married Josephine Hoy at St. Dominic's church, Haverstock Hill. Their marriage was blessed with a son, Michael, who inherited his father's love for foreign languages and is himself a teacher of difficult children. Michael has two lovely daughters, Maria Elizabeth (my namesake) and Francesca. It is not for me to speculate as to why Rory left the priesthood, but I think it is significant that the four close friends who went through the seminary together, and then went on to Cambridge and taught at St. Peter's School, all left the Priesthood. When their ordination class celebrated their silver jubilee, the four friends were the only ones missing.

Rory died quite unexpectedly after a visit to Lourdes. He ruptured his oesophagus and although he underwent a long operation, he died. My G.P. said it was a very rare condition but nearly always fatal. His requiem Mass was held at the Catholic church at Bushey. Several priests concelebrated and our son, John read one of the readings. The parish priest had no idea that Rory was a priest and was only told after his death.

My father retired from the Arsenal at the age of 67 years and initially he was somewhat lost. He built himself a greenhouse of wood brought from the Arsenal, and the garden at 33 Inglewood Road looked better than I had ever seen it. He was not a man without interests, unlike our neighbour, Mr. McKay. He was very good at painting landscapes (usually of Ireland), and he was a writer and a prolific reader. Mother spent a lot of time just talking to him as she understood how bad he was feeling. Fortunately this period did not last very long because just before our first wedding anniversary, on the 30th September 1967, I gave birth to twin girls, Helen and Catherine. This new addition to our family, that came rather late in the lives of my parents, gave both of them a new lease of life. Initially they came down to our house in Bexley every day. In a very short time they became experts at feeding and changing nappies and bringing up wind; and they turned their hands to anything I asked them to do. Disposable nappies were still something of a rarity, so Mother took over the washing and drying of the "terry" nappies.

Dad did the washing-up while I prepared the babies for their morning walk. He would then push them out in their lovely "Gold Cross" pram, walking through Bexley village and the surrounding roads. Being twins they attracted a certain amount of interest although we discovered that there were a number of other twins in Bexley at that time. By the time Dad brought the girls back, they would be fast asleep, so

After the Ceremony

we had to wait for them to wake up before giving them their dinner.

Mother usually went home about mid-day, but Dad stayed on to help with the feeding and when, after eighteen months I became pregnant again he stayed on to allow me to have a rest. John was only three months old when I became pregnant again, so Dad really became a full-time nurse. When Francis was a year old, we moved to Barnehurst to be nearer to my parents and within walking distance of St. Joseph's Primary School.

Dad died after a short illness on 27th October 1973 aged 76 years. He had been very upset by all the changes in the Church due to Vatican II, not to mention Rory leaving the priesthood. Mother had said, "It has happened, we have to accept it." And so they did, but I do know that Dad was inwardly heart-broken.

Mother and Dad had been childhood sweethearts and in all those years had never been apart. I never saw my mother cry and she re-built her life around our family. She continued to live at 33, Inglewood Road until she was 88 years old, when failing sight and the cold of a severe winter forced her to come and live with us.

Four years later when she became doubly incontinent, she moved to a residential home in Whitstable. We found it in the Southwark Catholic Directory and it was owned and run by a good Catholic Lady who cared for her until her death on 4th December 1994 at the age of 96 years. I never thought mother would live to be really old. She had always seemed to me to be rather delicate, until the birth of her grandchildren proved otherwise. Our eight grandchildren all know about great-grandmother McDermott. They quite often talk about her and I am sure that she and my Dad are looking down on them with great love.

Every book has to have an ending and these memoirs are no exception. When my friend Pamela disappeared from the scene, the little group of riders seemed to break up. Janet Gale was courting Denis O'Sullivan or she may even have been married by then. That only left Alf and Naomi and perhaps Josie Lyle. So for the first time in years I was free to do other things on Sunday. I joined the church choir and that meant attending choir practice and singing at the 10:30 Mass on Sunday and at Benediction in the afternoon. That was how my friendship with David started. I would invite him in to tea after Benediction and he would take me for a run in his car.

By the summer of 1965 we were definitely going out together, although not engaged and I tried to carry on as usual. This meant going for a holiday in Ireland, but somehow I had lost the taste for it and after a couple of days I came home. David says that when he went up into the choir-loft to take choir practice and knew I wouldn't be there, he felt a big "hole" (I am not quite sure where). Then, who should come running up the stairs but me. We were engaged just after Christmas that year and married the following October, 1966. And therein ends my story.

Theotokos Books Foyer Titles

Marthe Robin and the Foyers of Charity, by Martin Blake

This book looks at the life of Marthe Robin, the French mystic, who, with Fr Georges Finet, co-founded the Foyer of Charity community at Châteauneuf-de-Galaure in southeastern France in 1936. There are now 75 Foyer communities throughout the world, and their work involves a priest, the Father of the Foyer, giving 5 day retreats in silence, during which the members of the community look after the needs of the retreatants and pray for them.

With a Foreword by Mgr Keith Barltrop and a Preface by Stratford Caldecott

£7.95 paperback, £3.60 Kindle/ePub versions - 160 pages

For more details please visit:
http://www.theotokos.org.uk/pages/books/marthebook/marthebook.html

Christian Living: The Spirituality of the Foyers of Charity by Donal Anthony Foley

This book contains essential information about Marthe Robin and the Foyers of Charity, as well as chapters based on retreats given by Fr Michel Tierny, the Father of the Foyer of Charity at Courset, in France. These cover topics such as discipleship, prayer, silence, the sacraments, and more. With a foreword by the renowned Newman scholar, Fr Ian Ker, this is an excellent new guide to living a better Christian life.

£7.95 paperback, £3.60 Kindle/ePub versions - 160 pages

For more details please visit:
http://www.theotokos.org.uk/pages/books/foyerbook/foyerbook.html

For more details about Marthe Robin and the Foyers please visit:

http://www.foyers.org.uk/

Theotokos Books Marian Titles

Marian Apparitions, the Bible, and the Modern World

by Donal Anthony Foley
Foreword by Fr Aidan Nichols OP

Imprimatur from Bishop McMahon of Nottingham

ISBN 0852443137 - 374pp - £19.99

This is an in depth investigation into the major Marian apparitions that have occurred during the last five centuries. It relates them to secular happenings and important revolutionary events in Western history including the Reformation and the French and Russian Revolutions. It also argues that the major apparitions are not random or historically inconsequential events, but actually seem to follow a preordained plan, one intimately linked with the biblical Marian typology explored by the Church Fathers. In particular, this books looks at the importance of Fatima in the life of the Church, its links with the papacy, and its continuing relevance for the Third Millennium.

"With his Marian Apparitions, the Bible, and the Modern World, *Donal Foley has made a very important contribution to our understanding and appreciation of private revelations, in particular those of Our Lady. ... Not only ... scholars and believers, but the general public will find this volume informative and inspirational."*

- Fr. Peter M. Fehlner, F.I.

"Donal Foley has written a book with an extraordinary message."
- Fr Aidan Nichols OP

To order please visit:

www.theotokos.org.uk/pages/books/mariapps/mariapps.html

or: www.amazon.co.uk/exec/obidos/ASIN/0852443137/theotokoscath-21

or you can order via online booksellers or through your local bookseller.

Lightning Source UK Ltd.
Milton Keynes UK
UKHW010742210722
406179UK00001B/188